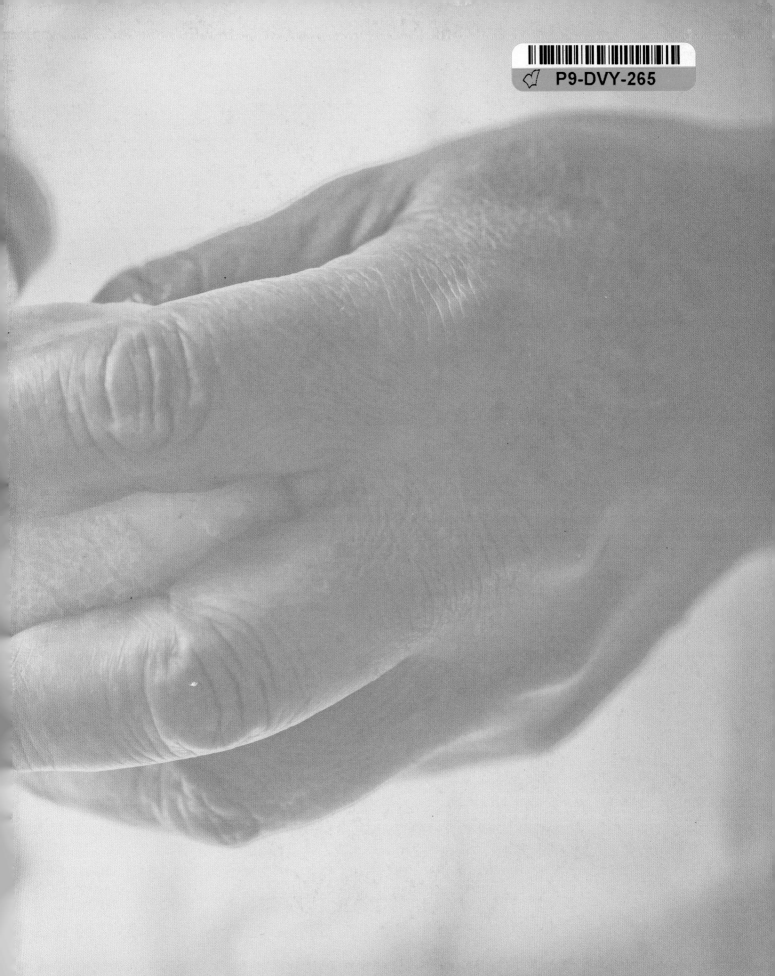

Vietnamese Home Cooking

Vietnamese Home Cooking

Charles Phan

Chef-Owner, The Slanted Door
with Jessica Battilana

Photography by Eric Wolfinger

TEN SPEED PRESS
Berkeley

Ten Speed Press and the Ten Speed Press colophon
are registered trademarks of Random House, Inc.

Library of Congress Cataloging-in-Publicaion Data
Phan, Charles.
    Vietnamese home cooking / Charles Phan, Chef-
Owner of The Slanted Door.
        p. cm.
1. Cooking, Vietnamese. I. Slanted Door (Restaurant)
II. Title.
    TX724.5.V5P54 2012
    641.59'295922—dc23

                                2012014119

ISBN: 978-1-60774-053-7
eISBN: 978-1-60774-385-9

Book design by Manual

Printed in China

10 9 8 7 6 5 4 3 2 1

For Dad and Ah Neng

Steaming

Braising

Frying

Glossary

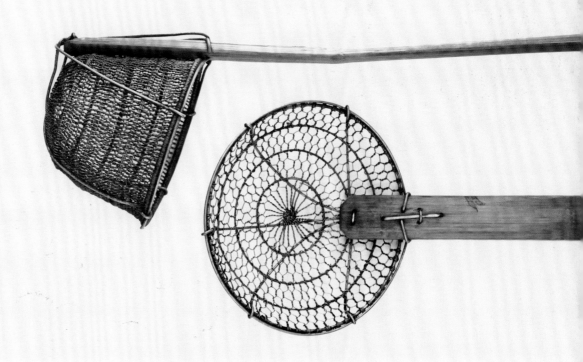

Preface
—

For years I have been asked to write a cookbook, and for years I would come up with excuses—I was opening a restaurant, or my wife was having a baby. But after three kids and six restaurants, I ran out of excuses.

When I finally decided to write a cookbook, I knew I didn't want it to simply be a collection of recipes, I wanted it to be rich with information. I wanted to introduce cooks to unfamiliar (but widely available) ingredients and expand their cooking repertoire by showing them new ways to treat familiar ingredients. I wanted to teach readers about clay pots and woks, about caramel sauce and lemongrass. And I wanted to share the fundamental flavors that make Vietnamese food so unique and, I think, so good.

My hope was—and is—that this book helps cooks understand the Vietnamese aesthetic, our way of cooking and eating.

The book is organized around fundamental cooking techniques, in the hope that by mastering these techniques you'll become a better, more confident cook. But this organization also reflects the way that Vietnamese people truly eat, building meals that include a stir-fried dish alongside something fried, along with a simple soup and a grilled piece of meat. Many of the recipes here can be served as main courses, but I encourage you to try preparing a meal in the Vietnamese-style, choosing dishes from several different chapters and serving them together as part of a family-style, multicourse meal. It's what we do at the restaurants, what I do at my house and what I'd encourage you to try in yours.

"Charles was trained as a potter and architect—it is only by accident that he turned out to be an extraordinary chef. To me he is first and foremost a craftsman, and it makes perfect sense that his first cookbook would be organized around technique— this is really the craft of preparing great food."

—T. Olle Lundberg, Charles' architect and drinking partner

You'll enjoy the recipes in this book all the more if you start thinking—and eating—like a Vietnamese person.

A Vietnamese meal, unlike a Western meal, is rarely just a single dish. More often, it's a collection of dishes—some served hot, others cool—that contain a mixture of textures and employ a variety of cooking techniques.

At home, I might pair a steamed whole fish or a clay pot with some stir-fried greens, or maybe some fried chicken wings. Rice is often served with the meal, but noodles usually come at the end, because they are so filling that eating them at the start of the meal would ruin your appetite. And though some dishes are served hot—like soups and braises—other things, like noodles, rolls, and dumplings—are perfectly good at room temperature.

Many of the recipes in this book are suggested as part of a multicourse meal. Choose a few from a variety of chapters and you'll be well on your way to eating in the Vietnamese style.

Introduction

—

I can still remember the menu: turkey, stuffing, sweet potatoes, green beans, gravy, cranberry sauce, and an apple pie. It was Thanksgiving 1978, and I had just cooked my first major meal in my family's small kitchen. I was fifteen years old and our family of ten—my parents, five siblings, and my aunt and uncle—had been living in America for only eleven months. We had left Vietnam three years earlier, in April 1975, just before the fall of Ho Chi Minh City. From there we went to Guam, where we spent two years before finally making our way to the United States.

I was the oldest of my siblings and the only one who spoke some English, so I set about trying to assimilate our family to our new life in America. There I was, a kid who had never even seen Brussels sprouts, attempting to create the most American of American meals for my Vietnamese family in our rental apartment in San Francisco's Chinatown. Thanksgiving didn't mean much to me, since I didn't know what was being celebrated, but big family feasts were familiar. I saw cooking Thanksgiving dinner as a way of fitting in, which as a poor, immigrant kid in uncool clothes who barely spoke English I desperately wanted to do. I'd gotten my hands on a copy of *Gourmet* magazine that featured a Thanksgiving feast and decided to make the entire menu, cooking it all on our white double-oven Wedgewood stove. My family didn't like the dinner. I remember them saying, "We'd rather eat Chinese food any day." Thank God I'd cooked rice to go with the gravy.

Both of my parents worked two jobs, so I cooked for our family throughout high school out of necessity, mixing my mother's traditional Vietnamese recipes with new American ingredients. Along the way, I taught myself some American classics, like chocolate cake and pancakes.

Although I have a growing family of restaurants, I consider myself a glorified home cook. The food that we serve at the restaurants is mostly my (and my family's) home cooking—like scrambled eggs with pork and chicken porridge—adapted for a restaurant, not the other way around. It is simple and direct cooking, and I think that's the reason we have so many return guests. The food is interesting without being challenging; it is simple, honest, and straightforward, yet incredibly flavorful. I see this cookbook as an extension of what we do at the restaurants. But it is also an extension of what I've done since I was a kid making great food that blends traditions, celebrates Asian recipes, and can be made in an American kitchen, where I have cooked my entire life.

This book is technique driven because I believe that's the best way to learn Vietnamese cooking. Each technique requires a unique skill set and equipment, but once you've mastered the fundamentals, making the dishes will become second nature. Technique, no matter how humble the dish, is important, whether you are wrapping spring rolls or making a crisp-skinned fried duck. Once you are at ease with techniques in these pages, you will be a better all-around cook of Vietnamese cuisine.

You will find recipes here that are so easy that I make them twice a week for my kids, like Ground Pork with Salted Fish (page 84); others that I make for special occasions, such as Fragrant Crispy Duck with Watercress (page 186); and still others that I eat when it's just me alone at home with a cold beer, like Fried Rice (page 144).

My customers have been asking me to write a cookbook for the last decade, but it has taken me that long to figure out what I wanted to say. At the restaurant, we have broken down the barriers for diners unfamiliar with the food of Vietnam. With this book, I am hoping to do the same for both home cooks and professional chefs. I see this volume as my opportunity to introduce and inspire readers to start and continue to cook flavorful and healthful Vietnamese food in their own kitchens. There is no mystery to the food I serve. My version of the Vietnamese dishes I grew up eating and the ones I serve at my restaurants are yours for the mastering, and this book will show you the way.

Soup

I grew up in the city of Đà Lat, which lies about 190 miles northeast of Ho Chi Minh City in the country's central highlands. In the late 1960s and early 1970s my siblings and I weren't allowed to go out in the streets alone because kids were being kidnapped and forced into the North Vietnamese army. We spent a lot of time inside our home, which was on the second floor above the general store my parents owned. When it was time for breakfast,

instead of going out for food, the food vendors would come to us. You could hear them before you saw them, noisely banging together bamboo sticks to get attention and announcing their wares with a shout. Imagine the Good Humor man, but instead of a truck it was a woman with a long bamboo pole across her shoulders. On one end hung a pot of hot stock and on the opposite end were all of the other ingredients for a bowl of pho: noodles, herbs and chiles, pieces of meat.

When we heard the call, we'd all rush to the window. Then, one at a time, we'd lower down the basket with an empty bowl and some money. The soup vendor would fill the bowl and we'd carefully lift it back up. Breakfast was served.

When you eat a bowl of soup in Vietnam, you experience almost everything, culinarily speaking, that the Vietnamese value. Although the number of soups in the Vietnamese repertoire is large, they all share a similar aesthetic. Stock is flavorful and light, never thickened and heavy. Every bowl includes a texturally interesting mix of soft ingredients (like noodles), crunchy elements (mung bean sprouts, fried shallots), and chewy bits (pieces of beef tendon, shredded chicken, spongy meatballs). And every bowl—be it a heartier noodle soup or a lighter first-course soup—is finished with aromatics: fresh herbs, toasted garlic, chile oil, chopped scallions, or even, as was once served to me at a food stall in Hanoi, the secretion from a gland of a specific variety of male beetle, which was dripped onto the surface of my chicken pho, forming a fragrant oil slick that perfumed each bite of the soup.

In Vietnam, there are two classes of soup: filling noodle soups that are most often eaten in the morning or for lunch

and are a meal unto themselves, and brothier, lighter soups that are typically eaten at the start of a multicourse meal, usually dinner. In the noodle-soup category is pho, one of the most well-known Vietnamese dishes outside Vietnam. Ask a Korean, Chinese, or American person what he or she knows about Vietnamese food and this soup will probably be the answer. The contrast of silky noodles with crunchy bean sprouts, the full-flavored broth enhanced with the addition of fresh herbs—makes it the perfect one-bowl meal.

There's a reason that most people in Vietnam buy noodle soups from a vendor. Putting together a bowl of soup isn't complicated, but it does require some effort.  You need a good, rich stock, which takes time to prepare. The meat, whether steamed chicken, stewed brisket, or shrimp-and-pork-filled wontons, must be cooked and at the ready. The noodles must be soaked, and a generous platter of herbs and sliced chiles needs to be prepared and offered alongside, so eaters can customize their bowls. Everyone always talks about being so busy, and making noodle soup isn't something for the busy person. But if you break up the work over a few days, and if you try to always keep stock in your freezer, you'll get into a routine, and a bowl of soup will never be too far out of reach.

When making soup at home, it's important to prewarm the serving bowls and to bring the stock up to a full boil before ladling it into the bowls so that it's piping hot when served. In the case of noodle soups, the order of assembly is important: noodles are put in the bowl first, next the meat, and finally the stock is ladled over the top. Herb garnishes and lime wedges are served alongside—and never, ever in the bowl. A bowl of soup should be hot from start to finish, and you should eat it quickly, before it cools or, in the case of noodle soup, before the noodles overcook. And yes, slurping is okay.

The purpose of the brothier, noodleless soups is to stimulate the appetite, much the way a bowl of miso soup is served before a Japanese meal, or a crystal-clear consommé begins a classic French dinner. These soups are often little more than stock—fish, chicken, or beef—with a few vegetables or bits of meat stirred in. They are never blended, never creamy, and never thick. Vietnamese cuisine has no equivalent to cream of broccoli soup or minestrone.

When I was growing up, every meal began with one of these brothier soups. My own record isn't as good, but when I start a meal with a soup, the whole dinner feels more balanced.

In this chapter, you'll learn how to make both categories of soups. Some will be familiar, like Wonton Noodle Soup (page 14). Others, like the Hot and Sour Shrimp Soup (page 25) with its tamarind, pineapple, and shrimp, will probably be like nothing you've had before. Master the soups in this chapter and you will have mastered one of the most fundamental parts of the Vietnamese diet.

About Stock

—

Although these recipes for chicken and beef stock are hardly the sexiest, most exciting recipes in the book, they are some of the most important. If you are planning to make soup, or thinking about some of the recipes in the braising chapter, you'll be ahead of the game if you already have stock in the freezer. It's not worth making pho with canned stock, so don't even bother. A flavorful broth is absolutely key to the success of the recipe.

It takes time to make good stock, but it's mostly lazy, inactive time: a pot bubbling away on the stove for the better part of the day, while you watch the Masters at Augusta. Set aside a day of the week as your stock making day, and make two batches at the same time.

A classic French stock is made by first roasting bones in the oven to draw out impurities. But because most Vietnamese kitchens don't have ovens, Vietnamese cooks always first blanch the bones briefly in boiling water, then rinse them thoroughly with fresh water before simmering in more water to make stock. The two techniques, though quite different, achieve the same goal: a clear stock free of impurities. And while a French stock draws roasted flavor and color from the browned bones, a Vietnamese stock is flavored and colored by roasted onions and garlic, which were traditionally blackened over an open flame. Today, we roast the onion and garlic in the oven.

Pork Stock

—

This pork stock is light in color but rich in flavor. You can use a mixture of any type of pork bones, including knuckle or neck, but do try and find a trotter—it will enhance both the taste and texture of the finished stock.

   I always encourage buying humanely raised pork and think it's especially important here. Good quality pork (and pork bones) will give you a broth that's meaty and pure. Lesser-quality so-called "commodity pork" results in a stock that has an ammoniated, unpleasant flavor.

- 5 pounds meaty pork bones
- 1 trotter, split lengthwise (ask your butcher to do this)
- 1 large yellow onion, peeled and coarsely chopped
- 1 teaspoon whole white peppercorns
- 1 tablespoon kosher salt

Makes about 4 quarts

1.
Blanch the bones: To ensure the pot is large enough to blanch the bones without boiling over, put the bones in the pot and add water to cover by 1 inch. Then remove the bones and bring the water to a boil. When it is at a rolling boil, add half of the pork bones, return the water to a boil, and boil for 5 minutes.

2.
With a spider or tongs, remove the first batch of bones from the water and place in a colander. Return the water to a boil and repeat with remaining pork bones. When all the bones have been blanched, rinse under cold running water. Rinse the pot and return the bones to the pot.

3.
Add the trotter, onion, white peppercorns, salt, and 6 quarts of cold water to the pot and bring to a boil over high heat, skimming off any scum that forms on the surface. Lower the heat so the liquid is at a gentle simmer and simmer for 2 hours, skimming as needed to remove any scum that forms on the surface.

4.
Remove from the heat and, using a spider or a slotted spoon, discard the large solids. Strain the stock through a fine-mesh sieve into a large container, let sit for a few minutes (or refrigerate overnight), then skim most of the fat from the surface (leave some, as it gives the stock a better flavor and mouth-feel). Use immediately, or let cool completely, then transfer to practical-size airtight container and refrigerate for up to 3 days or freeze for up to 3 months.

Soup

Chicken Stock

—

Don't underestimate the power of chicken stock. Each time my wife was in labor with one of our children, I brought pints of frozen stock to the hospital. Now it is a Slanted Door tradition for pregnant staff members. Nutritious and easy to digest, it's a perfect restorative, whether you're giving birth or just under the weather. You will note that the recipe does not contain carrots or celery. We only use roasted onion, ginger, and a small amount of palm sugar to sweeten the stock.

Adding dried squid, scallops, or shrimp to chicken stock is common in Asia. The "secret" ingredient in our chicken stock is dried sea worms. Called *sa sung* in Vietnamese, they resemble overgrown earthworms and add a savory note to the broth. They can be difficult to find in the United States (though they can be found in Chinatown) so this recipe does not call for them. Not to worry; it's delicious without them. Don't simmer the stock too vigorously, or it will end up cloudy.

- 1 large yellow onion, unpeeled
- 3-inch piece fresh ginger, unpeeled
- 7 pounds bony chicken parts such as back, wings, and necks
- 1¼ tablespoons kosher salt
- 1¼ ounces light brown palm sugar (see page 208) or 2 tablespoons light brown sugar

Makes about 5½ quarts

1.
Preheat the oven to 350°F. Place the onion and ginger on a rimmed baking sheet and roast for about 1 hour, until the onion is soft and beginning to ooze. Remove from the oven and let the onion and ginger cool until they can be handled. Peel the onion and cut in half. Slice the unpeeled ginger into ¼-inch-thick coins.

2.
While the onion and ginger are roasting, blanch the chicken bones: To ensure the pot is large enough to blanch the bones without boiling over, put the bones in the pot and add water to cover by 1 inch. Then remove the bones, set aside, and bring the water to a boil.

3.
When it is at a rolling boil, add the bones, return the water to a boil and boil for 3 minutes. Drain the bones into a colander and rinse under cold running water. Rinse the pot and return the rinsed bones to the pot.

4.
Add the onion halves, ginger slices, salt, sugar, and 8 quarts fresh water to the pot and bring to a boil over high heat, skimming off any scum that forms on the surface. Lower the heat so the liquid is at a gentle simmer and simmer for 4 hours, skimming as needed to remove any scum that forms on the surface.

5.
Remove the pot from the heat and, using a spider or a slotted spoon, remove and discard the large solids. Strain the stock through a fine-mesh sieve into a large container, let sit for a few minutes (or refrigerate overnight), then skim most of the fat from the surface (leave some, as it gives the stock a better flavor and mouthfeel). Season to taste with salt.

6.
Use immediately, or let cool completely, then transfer to practical-size airtight containers and refrigerate for up to 3 days or freeze for up to 3 months.

Beef Stock

—

At the restaurants, we use a variety of different beef bones for our stock because we think the combination gives it the best flavor. Unlike the shank and neck bones and oxtail, the marrowbones don't get blanched. That's because the hot water would melt the marrow, and since you discard the blanching liquid, you'd be throwing all that delicious flavor down the drain. If you can get bones from grass-fed beef, use them here. The flavor is probably most similar to the beef available in Vietnam.

- 1 large yellow onion, unpeeled
- 3-inch piece fresh ginger
- 2 pounds oxtails, cut in 2- to 3-inch pieces
- 2 pounds beef neck bones
- 2 pounds beef shank bones
- 2 pounds beef marrowbones
- 1 ounce light brown palm sugar (see page 208), or 2 tablespoons light brown sugar
- 1 tablespoon kosher salt
- 1 teaspoon ground white pepper
- 3-inch piece Chinese cinnamon (see page 203)
- 1 whole star anise pod (see page 211)
- 1 whole clove
- 1 black cardamom pod (optional; see page 203)

Makes about 6 quarts

1.
Preheat the oven to 350°F. Place the onion and ginger on a rimmed baking sheet and roast until the onion is soft and beginning to ooze, about 1 hour. Remove from the oven and let the onion and ginger cool until they can be handled. Peel the onion and cut in half. Slice the unpeeled ginger into ¼-inch-thick coins.

2.
While the onion and ginger are roasting, blanch the bones: To ensure the pot is large enough to blanch the bones without boiling over, put the bones, in the pot and add water to cover by 1 inch. Then remove the bones and bring the water to a boil. When it is at a rolling boil, add the oxtails, neck bones, and shanks. Return the water to a boil and boil for 3 minutes. Drain the contents of the pot into a colander and rinse under cold running water. Rinse the pot and return the rinsed oxtails, neck bones, and shanks to the pot. Add the marrowbones.

3.
Add the onion halves, ginger slices, sugar, salt, and 8 quarts fresh water to the pot and bring to a boil over high heat, skimming off any scum that forms on the surface. Lower the heat so the liquid is at a gentle simmer and simmer for 4 hours, skimming as needed to remove any scum that forms on the surface.

4.
Add the pepper, cinnamon, star anise, clove, and cardamom and continue cooking, skimming occasionally, for 1 hour longer.

5.
Remove from the heat and and, using a spider or a slotted spoon, discard the large solids. Strain the stock through a fine-mesh sieve into a large container, let sit for a few minutes (or refrigerate overnight), then skim most of the fat from the surface (leave some, as it gives the stock a better flavor and mouthfeel). Use immediately, or let cool completely, then transfer to practical-size airtight containers and refrigerate for up to 3 days or freeze for up to 3 months.

Soup

Pho Gá: Chicken Noodle Soup

—

I eat pho—chicken or beef—almost every morning at the restaurant. It's also the first thing I eat when I go back to Vietnam. My family left Vietnam when I was twelve years old, and eighteen years passed before I returned. On my first trip back, I landed in Ho Chi Minh City in the morning from an overnight flight. It was disorienting to disembark from the plane into the humid day, stepping into a country that was both intensely familiar and also a distant memory. I went straight to a coffee shop, a noisy shoebox of a space where men were talking over coffee and the owner was dispensing bowl after bowl of pho. I was back in Vietnam.

Bowls of pho are the hamburgers of Vietnam: incredibly popular, eaten every day by a majority of the population, young and old. In the mornings in Ho Chi Minh City, you see commuters sitting astride their parked mopeds, slurping down a bowl before they continue on to work.

Every pho place serves the soup with a plate of garnishes: *rau ram*, mint, Thai basil, slices of jalapeño chile, mung bean sprouts, lime wedges, and sometimes fried shallots or Chinese Doughnuts (page 48). The trick is to add a little bit of each item as you eat your way through the bowl, not to dump them in all at once. You want the herbs to maintain their fragrance, the bean sprouts to stay crunchy—it's all about aroma and texture, and if you add too much too soon, you'll end up with black herbs and soft sprouts, which defeats the whole purpose.

- 1 (3-pound) whole chicken (see page 101)
- 6 whole scallions
- 1 thumb-sized piece of ginger, crushed
- 1 tablespoon kosher salt
- 3 quarts chicken stock (see page 6)
- Fish sauce, for seasoning
- 1 (16-ounce) package dried rice vermicelli (see page 12), cooked according to package directions
- 1 bunch scallions, trimmed and thinly sliced (about 1 cup)
- 1 bunch cilantro, chopped (about 1½ cups)
- Crispy fried shallots (see page 9)

Garnishes
- Thai basil sprigs (see page 213)
- Mung bean sprouts (see page 207)
- Limes, cut into wedges
- Jalapeño chiles, stemmed and thinly sliced into rings

Serves 6

1.
Bring a large pot of water to a boil over high heat. Add the chicken, scallions, ginger, and salt and boil for 15 minutes, then turn off the heat, cover the pot and let stand for 15 minutes. If your chicken is larger than 3 pounds, let stand 10 minutes longer.

2.
Just before the chicken is ready, prepare a large ice-water bath. When the chicken is done, remove it from the pot (discarding the cooking liquid) and immediately submerge it in the ice-water bath, which will stop the cooking and give the meat a firmer texture. Let stand 20 minutes, until the chicken is cool enough to handle easily, remove from the water, and pat dry. Pull the chicken meat from the bones, discarding the bones and skin. Shred the meat with your fingers; you should have about 4 cups. (This step can be done a day ahead.)

3.
In a large saucepan, bring the stock to a boil over high heat. Taste for seasoning and add fish sauce, if needed.

4.
To ready the garnishes, arrange the basil, bean sprouts, lime wedges, and chiles on a platter and place on the table.

5.
Divide the rice noodles evenly among warmed soup bowls. Top each serving with about ¾ cup of the shredded chicken, then divide the scallions and cilantro evenly among the bowls. Ladle the hot stock over the top, dividing it evenly, and sprinkle with the fried shallots. Serve immediately, accompanied with the platter of garnishes.

Crispy Fried Shallots
—

Crispy fried shallots are an essential condiment in Vietnam. They turn up in soups and on salads, sprinkled onto dumplings as a garnish, and minced and added to meatballs. Crispy, sweet, and salty, they are indispensible. You may want to make double batches, as people have a hard time resisting the urge to snack on them. Strain the oil you used to fry the shallots and use it in other recipes or to fry more shallots. The strained oil, called shallot oil, will keep, refrigerated, for several weeks. The shallots should be used the same day they are fried.

- 2 cups thinly sliced shallots (about 4 large shallots)
- 2 cups canola oil

Makes 1 cup fried shallots

1.
In a small saucepan, heat the oil over medium-high until it registers 275°F on a deep-fry thermometer. Add the shallots and cook, stirring, until light golden brown, about 8 minutes. Using a slotted spoon, transfer the shallots to a paper towel-lined plate to drain.

2.
Increase the heat to high and place a fine-mesh sieve over a heat-proof bowl. When the oil registers 350°F on the deep-fry thermometer, add the once fried shallots and cook just until they are crispy and well-browned, about 1–2 seconds, watching carefully so the shallots don't burn.

3.
Immediately pour the oil and shallots through the sieve to stop the cooking, then transfer to shallots to a paper towel-lined plate to drain. Reserve the oil for another use. The shallots will keep, stored in an airtight container, for 1 day, but they're best the day they are made.

Pho Bò: Beef Noodle Soup
—

One of my favorite spots for beef pho is Pho Hoa in Ho Chi Minh City (pictured opposite). Everyone knows this place, and when I'm there I order the special, which is loaded with meat, including tripe, meatball, and tendon.

Pho bò usually contains two or more cuts of beef, often cooked brisket and raw slices of top round, along with tendon. But in North Vietnam the soup only contains slices of raw beef. As I have already mentioned, in Vietnam, bowls of noodle soup are built from the bowl up—first the noodles, then the meat, with hot stock ladled over at the last minute and garnishes served alongside. This is especially important with Pho bò because the beef is added to the bowl raw and the heat from the stock cooks it just enough. Hoisin sauce and Sriracha sauce often accompany bowls of Pho bò, but they should never be added to the stock itself because they will ruin the delicate, beefy flavor. Instead, retrieve pieces of meat from the soup and drag them through the sauces just before eating. If you want a spicier broth, add more jalapeño slices. To slice the raw beef paper-thin, freeze the whole piece for 15 minutes before slicing, then pound the slices with a meat mallet or the back of a heavy knife.

- 1 pound beef brisket
- 3 quarts beef stock (see page 7)
- Fish sauce (see page 36), for seasoning
- 1 (16-ounce) package dried wide rice noodles (see page 12), cooked according to package directions
- 12 ounces beef top round, thinly sliced
- 1 bunch scallions, trimmed and thinly sliced (about 1 cup)

Garnishes
- Thai basil sprigs (see page 213)
- Mung bean sprouts (see page 207)
- Lime wedges
- Jalapeño chiles, stemmed and thinly sliced into rings
- Sriracha sauce
- Hoisin sauce

Serves 6

1.
Place the brisket in a large pot and add the stock. Bring to a boil over high heat, then lower the heat until the liquid is at a vigorous simmer. Cook the brisket for 30 to 45 minutes, until cooked through. To check for doneness, remove the brisket from the pot to a plate and poke with the tip of a chopstick; the juices should run clear.

2.
Just before the brisket is ready, prepare an ice-water bath. When the brisket is done, remove it from the pot, reserving the cooking liquid, and immediately submerge it in the ice-water bath, which will stop the cooking and give the meat a firmer texture. When the brisket is completely cool, remove from the water, pat dry, and thinly slice against the grain. Set aside.

3.
Return the stock to a boil over high heat. Taste for seasoning and add fish sauce if needed.

4.
To ready the garnishes, arrange the basil, bean sprouts, lime wedges, and chiles on a platter and place on the table and put the Sriracha and hoisin sauces alongside.

5.
Divide the cooked rice noodles evenly among warmed soup bowls. Top with the brisket slices and then with the raw beef slices, dividing them evenly. Ladle the hot stock over the top, dividing it evenly, and top with the scallions. Serve immediately, accompanied with the platter of garnishes.

Noodles
—

Noodles are an integral part of the Vietnamese diet, and there is an astonishing variety of types sold fresh in every market in Vietnam. These same fresh noodles are available in some cities in the States, but not everywhere. Dried noodles, which can be found readily in many stores and online, are a fine substitute.

Cellophane Noodles

Called *mien* in Vietnamese, and also known as glass noodles and bean thread noodles, cellophane noodles are typically used in fillings, like the buns on page 82 or the stuffed squid on page 156, or in delicate noodle stir-fries. In the United States, they are only available dried, in various-size packages. Check the list of ingredients. You want to find only mung beans and water on the label. Beware of brands that contain other ingredients, as the noodles are usually brittle and of poor quality. Rehydrate cellophane noodles before using by soaking in hot water to cover for 10 to 15 minutes.

Rice Noodles

There are two basic types of rice noodles, flat and round. The flat noodles are traditionally used in pho. You can find them dried (and in some places, fresh) in thin, medium, and wide widths, but the narrowest ones are best for soup. They are usually sold in 14- or 16-ounce packages. Before adding the noodles to soups or stir-fries, boil them in a generous amount of unsalted water until they are tender yet still have some bite, then drain and rinse with cold water. If you are using fresh noodles, they do not need to be precooked.

Round rice noodles, called bun, are also available in various widths, both fresh and dried. The thinnest round rice noodles, also called vermicelli, are used in spring rolls (page 44); either thin or wide round rice noodles form the base of noodle bowls (page 170). For a fun weekend project, try making fresh rice noodles at home (page 172).

Bún Bò Hue (page 16) is traditionally made with round rice noodles that resemble spaghetti. They are available dried in various thicknesses, either as straight sticks or in skeins. If the package specifies size, look for "large" or "extra large." These noodles should be boiled in a generous amount of unsalted water until they are tender yet still have some bite, then drained and rinsed with cold water. The cool noodles are added to bowls, then the hot stock is poured over. Homemade fresh rice noodles can be substituted (page 172).

Egg Noodles

Although you can buy dried egg noodles, fresh ones are much better and are stocked in both supermarkets and Asian groceries. They are often labeled "Chinese egg noodles" and are available in a handful of thicknesses. For soups and stir-fries, I think the thinnest type (¹⁄₁₆ inch) is best. As with rice noodles, egg noodles should be boiled in a generous amount of unsalted water, then drained and rinsed with cold water. Uncooked packages of fresh egg noodles can be frozen for up to 3 months, so buy a few packages at one time. Thaw them in the refrigerator completely before boiling.

Wonton Noodle Soup

—

After Pho Gá, this is probably the most popular soup on The Slanted Door menu. It's what you might call "fully loaded": Chinese egg noodles (and never rice noodles), wontons filled with a mix of pork and shrimp, and slices of braised pork.

Vietnam has a large number of Chinese immigrants, and an even larger number of people who were born and raised in Vietnam but are ethnically Chinese. These are the people who introduced this iconic Chinese soup to Vietnam. In the States, wontons are often overstuffed—they look like meatballs with a skin wrapped around them. But the word wonton translates as "swallowing cloud," and the amount of filling should really be about the size of a small marble, an accent to the silky wrapper. If all you have ever eaten is Chinese takeout wonton soup, try this.

Pork and Shrimp Wontons

- 8 ounces shrimp peeled, deveined, and finely chopped
- 4 ounces ground pork
- ⅓ cup fried shallots (see page 9)
- 3 tablespoons shallot oil (see page 9)
- 1⅓ cup finely chopped fresh water chestnuts (see page 213) or jicama (see page 206)
- ⅓ cup finely chopped black trumpet mushrooms
- 2 tablespoons finely chopped fresh cilantro
- 2 tablespoons finely chopped scallion, white and light green parts only
- 1 tablespoon plus 1 teaspoon oyster sauce (see page 214)
- 1 tablespoon sesame seeds, toasted and ground to a coarse powder
- 1 tablespoon finely minced shallot
- 1 tablespoon fish sauce (see page 36)
- 2 teaspoons toasted sesame oil
- Pinch of freshly ground black pepper
- 50 square wonton wrappers (1-pound package)
- Cornstarch, for dusting

- 4 quarts chicken or pork stock (see pages 5 and 6)
- 1 pound fresh thin egg noodles (see page 13)
- Lo Soi Braised Pork (see page 113), thinly sliced
- ½ cup chopped scallions, dark green part only
- ½ cup chopped fresh cilantro
- ½ cup fried shallots (see page 9)
- Pork cracklings, optional (see page 19)

Serves 6

1.
To make the wontons, in a bowl, combine the shrimp, pork, fried shallots, shallot oil, water chestnuts, mushrooms, cilantro, scallion, oyster sauce, sesame seeds, raw shallot, fish sauce, and sesame oil and mix well. The mixture will be loose.

2.
To form each wonton, place a wonton wrapper on a work surface and place ½ teaspoon filling in the center. Pull the wonton wrapper up and around the filling to make a purse, twisting the wrapper slightly to enclose the meat. Transfer the finished wonton to a baking sheet or large tray lightly dusted with cornstarch.

3.
Repeat until you have used up all of the filling. The wontons can be made a day ahead; if making ahead, dust the wontons generously with cornstarch and transfer to a parchment-lined baking sheet. Tightly cover with plastic wrap and refrigerate. They can also be frozen for up to 1 month: arrange them on a parchment-lined baking sheet, cover, and freeze until frozen solid, then transfer to resealable plastic storage bags or other airtight containers and return to the freezer. Do not thaw before cooking.

4.
In a large saucepan, bring the stock to a vigorous simmer. Bring a large pot of water to a rapid boil over high heat.

5.
Add the noodles to the boiling water and cook for about 1 minute, until they are tender yet still have some bite. Drain the noodles and divide them among warmed soup bowls. Top the noodles with the sliced Lo Soi pork, dividing them evenly. Add the wontons to the simmering stock and cook for 3 to 5 minutes, until they float.

6.
When the wontons are ready, using a spider or a slotted spoon, transfer them to the bowls, dividing them evenly. Ladle the hot stock into the bowls and garnish with the scallion, cilantro, fried shallots, and cracklings. Serve immediately.

Bún Bò Hue

—

The mention of Hue, a city in central Vietnam, brings up many conflicted memories for me. It was the site of the Battle of Hue, one of the longest and deadliest battles of the Tet Offensive, which began in January 1968, and of the Vietnam War. Although I was just a kid when the fighting took place, the stories that I heard about it during my childhood were frightening.

Hue was the imperial capital of Vietnam for nearly a century and a half, until 1945, and many of the most sophisticated and interesting dishes in the Vietnamese repertoire originated in the region, including this classic spicy beef soup. The light stock, which is made with beef and pork bones, is scented with lots of lemongrass and shrimp paste. Any rice noodle can be used here, but the usual choice is the round rice noodle that resembles spaghetti (see page 172). In Vietnam, the soup is often served with cubes of coagulated pig's blood, like the bowl pictured opposite.

Stock
- 2 pounds oxtail, cut into 2- to 3-inch pieces (ask your butcher to do this)
- 2 pounds beef shank bones, cut into 2- to 3-inch pieces (ask your butcher to do this)
- 2 pounds pork neck bones
- 2 pounds beef marrowbones, cut into 2- to 3-inch pieces (ask your butcher to do this)
- 1 pound beef brisket
- 8 lemongrass stalks

Soup
- 1½ teaspoons red pepper flakes
- 1 teaspoon annatto seeds (see page 202), ground
- ¼ cup plus 2 tablespoons canola oil
- 1 cup sliced shallots (2 extra-large shallots)
- 1 teaspoon minced garlic
- ¼ cup finely chopped lemongrass (see page 207)
- 2 teaspoons shrimp paste (see page 215)
- 2 teaspoons kosher salt
- 2 teaspoons sugar
- 1 (14-ounce) package dried round rice noodles, cooked according to package directions, or 3 pounds fresh rice noodles (see recipe page 172)

Garnishes
- Thai basil sprigs (see page 213)
- Perilla leaves (see page 208)
- Thinly sliced green or red cabbage
- Lemon wedges
- Lime wedges
- Thinly sliced yellow onion

Serves 6

1.
Make the stock: to ensure the pot is large enough to blanch the bones without boiling over, put the bones in the pot and add water to cover by 1 inch. Then remove the bones and set aside.

2.
Bring the water to a boil. When it is at a rolling boil, add the oxtails, beef shank, and pork bones. Return the water to a boil and boil for 3 minutes. Drain the bones into a colander and rinse under cold running water. Rinse the pot and return the rinsed oxtails, neck bones, and shanks to the pot. Add the marrowbones and brisket.

3.
Cut off the pale, fleshy part (the bottom 4 inches) of each lemongrass stalk and discard the leafy tops. Crush the lemongrass with the side of a cleaver or the bottom of a heavy pan and add it to the pot. Add 8 quarts fresh water and bring to a boil over high heat. Lower the heat so the liquid is at a simmer and skim off any scum that rises to the surface.

4.
After 45 minutes, ready an ice-water bath, then check the brisket for doneness by using the chopstick test: transfer the brisket to a plate and poke it with a chopstick; the juices should run clear. If they do not, return the brisket to the pot and continue cooking, checking again in 10 minutes. When the brisket is done, remove it from the pot (reserving the cooking liquid) and immediately submerge it in the ice-water bath, which will stop the cooking and give the meat a firmer texture. When the brisket is completely cool, remove from the water, pat dry, and refrigerate.

5.
Continue to simmer the stock for another 2 hours, skimming as needed to remove any scum that forms on the surface. Remove from the heat and remove and discard the large solids. Strain through a fine-mesh sieve into a large saucepan. Skim most of the fat from the surface of the stock (leave some, as it gives the stock a better flavor and mouthfeel). Return the stock to a simmer over medium heat.

6.
In a spice grinder or
mortar and pestle, grind
the red pepper flakes
and annatto seeds into a
coarse powder. In a fry-
ing pan, heat the oil over
medium heat. Add the
ground red pepper flakes
and annatto seeds and
cook, stirring, for
10 seconds. Add the shal-
lots, garlic, lemongrass,
and shrimp paste and
cook, stirring, for 2 minutes more, until the mix-
ture is aromatic and the
shallots are just begin-
ning to soften.

7.
Add the contents of the
frying pan to the simmer-
ing stock along with the
salt and sugar and simmer
for 20 minutes. Taste and
adjust the seasoning with
salt and sugar.

8.
To ready the garnishes,
arrange the basil, perilla,
cabbage, lemon and lime
wedges, and onion slices
on a platter and place on
the table. Thinly slice the
brisket against the grain.
Divide the cooked noodles
among warmed soup bowls,
then divide the brisket
slices evenly among the
bowls, placing them on
top of the noodles. Ladle
the hot stock over the
noodles and beef and serve
immediately, accompa-
nied with the platter of
garnishes.

Bánh Canh: Pig's Knuckle Soup

—

I know, I know: pig's knuckle soup. For some that doesn't sound good, but don't let it scare you. Trust me—it is one of the purest, simplest soups in Vietnam, with a clear, full-flavored pork stock and a wonderful mix of textures.

The literal translation of *bánh canh* is "cake soup," which probably refers to the thick, chewy noodles made from tapioca starch or rice flour that are the star ingredient of this otherwise simple soup. Many variations of the soup exist, including one made with river crab, but the noodles are a constant in all of them. The noodles are easy to make (see recipe on following page), but if you don't want to make them, you can find packages of dried bánh canh noodles or substitute fresh udon noodles. When ordering your pig's knuckle, or trotter, ask for the front leg, which is more tender than the back.

- 1 large yellow onion, unpeeled
- 4 pounds pork neck bones
- 1 (2- to 3-pound) pork knuckle (preferably from the front leg), cut crosswise into 6 slices each about ½ inch thick (ask your butcher to do this)
- Fish sauce (see page 36) and/or kosher salt, for seasoning
- 1 (14-ounce) package dried *bánh canh* noodles, 1 pound fresh udon noodles, or fresh homemade *bánh canh* noodles (see opposite)

Garnishes
- Thai basil sprigs (see page 213)
- Mung bean sprouts (see page 207)
- Thinly sliced scallions, white and light green parts only
- Coarsely chopped fresh cilantro

Serves 6

1.
Preheat the oven to 350°F. Place the onion on a small rimmed baking sheet or pie pan and roast for about 1 hour, until soft and beginning to ooze. Remove from the oven and let the onion cool until it can be handled. Peel the onion and cut in half.

2.
While the onion is roasting, make the stock. To ensure the pot is large enough to blanch the bones without boiling over, put the bones in the pot and add water to cover by 1 inch. Then remove the bones and bring the water to a boil. When it is at a rolling boil, add the neck bones and knuckle slices, return the water to a boil and boil for 3 minutes. Drain the contents of the pot into a colander and rinse under cold running water. Rinse the pot and return the rinsed neck bones—but not the knuckle—to the pot.

3.
Add the onion halves and 8 quarts fresh water to the pot and bring to a boil over high heat. Lower the heat so the liquid is at a simmer and skim off any scum that forms on the surface. Simmer for 2½ hours, skimming as needed to remove any scum that forms on the surface.

4.
Add the pork knuckle and continue to simmer for about 30 minutes longer, until the knuckle is tender. The meat will still cling to the bone a bit but should be easy to chew. Cut off a small piece to test for doneness. Taste the stock and season to taste with fish sauce and/or salt.

5.
Bring the stock to a boil, add the noodles, and cook until they are tender yet still have some bite, according to package directions. If using udon noodles, cook only until warmed through, about 3 minutes. Meanwhile, to ready the garnishes, arrange the basil, bean sprouts, scallions, and cilantro on a platter and place on the table.

6.
Drain the noodles and divide them evenly among warmed soup bowls. Top each serving of noodles with a piece of pork knuckle. Ladle the hot stock over the noodles and pork and serve immediately, accompanied with the platter of garnishes.

Pork Cracklings

—

We sprinkle these crispy cubes of pork fat as a garnish on the Wonton Noodle Soup (see page 14). You should be able to get a nice square of solid fat from your butcher; freezing the fat briefly before dicing it makes it easier to get nice clean squares. The cracklings should be used the same day they are made.

- 8 ounces pork fat, in 1 piece
- 2 cups canola oil

Makes a scant ⅛ cup

1.
Place the pork fat in the freezer until well chilled but not frozen solid, about 1 hour. With a sharp knife, dice the pork into ¼-inch cubes.

2.
Pour the oil into a heavy-bottomed saucepan and heat over medium heat to 225°F on a deep-frying thermometer. Carefully add pork fat to oil and fry, stirring occasionally, adjusting the heat as necessary to maintain the oil temperature at 225°F, until the pork fat turns a deep golden brown, about 30 minutes.

3.
With a slotted spoon, transfer the cracklings to a paper towel–lined baking sheet. Let cool 20 minutes. (The pork fat can be prepared to this point up to 3 days before you plan to serve it; store in an airtight container in the refrigerator.)

4.
Reheat the oil over medium-high heat to 350°F on the thermometer. Return the once-fried cracklings to the oil and fry for 2 minutes. With a slotted spoon, transfer to a baking sheet lined with clean paper towels to drain.

Bánh Canh Noodles

—

- 8 ounces wheat starch, plus more for dusting
- 2 tablespoons tapioca starch
- 1½ teaspoons canola oil
- 1¼ cups boiling water

Makes 6 cups

1.
In the bowl of an electric mixer fitted with a paddle attachment, combine the wheat and tapioca starches. In a large measuring cup, combine the oil and water.

2.
Turn the mixer to low and pour water mixture in a slow steady stream over the dry ingredients. When it has all been added, increase speed to medium and mix until you have a thick, sticky dough.

3.
Turn dough out onto a work surface lightly dusted with wheat starch. Knead 5 minutes, adding just enough wheat starch as you knead to keep the dough from sticking to your hands and your work surface.

4.
Divide dough into 6 equal pieces and cover with plastic wrap. Working with one piece at a time, roll dough into a snake about ½ inch thick and 12 inches long. Using a sharp knife, cut into ½ inch pieces.

5.
On an unfloured surface, using the heel of your hand, roll each piece out into 2-inch lengths, slightly fatter in the middles and tapered at both ends. Transfer finished noodles to a tray or baking sheet dusted with wheat starch. Repeat until you have used all of the dough.

6.
Pour water into a wok or stockpot and set one tier of a two-tiered steamer in the wok or on the rim of the stockpot. Make sure the water does not touch the bottom of the steamer. Remove the steamer and bring the water to a boil over high heat.

7.
Line each tier of the steamer with a round of parchment paper, cut to fit. Spread noodles on each tier of the steamer in a single layer (you may have to cook the noodles in batches), then place over the boiling water. Cover and steam 12 to 15 minutes, until the noodles are cooked through and have a springy texture.

8.
Let noodles cool completely. You can use immediately or cover and refrigerate for up to 3 days.

Cháo: Chicken Rice Porridge

—

This is the breakfast of champions, Vietnamese style! *Cháo*, called congee in English, *jook* in Cantonese, *zhou* in Mandarin, *kanji* in Tamil, and more, depending on which country you are in, is one of the simplest recipes in the Asian repertoire. The most basic version is made with white rice and water, simmered together until the rice breaks down and the mixture thickens. Other versions call for red rice, brown rice, or starchy short-grain rice. Some have meat and bits of fish cooked in them; others are left plain and are garnished at the table. The amount of time you simmer the rice in the water—from 20 minutes to 2 hours—determines the final texture of your porridge.

In the South, there is a particular style of porridge where the rice is cooked in a large quantity of rich stock just until tender, but not thick. It's typically served with meat and ginger dipping sauce on the side.

- 1 (3-pound) whole chicken (see page 101)
- 6 whole scallions
- Thumb-sized piece fresh ginger, crushed
- 1 tablespoon kosher salt, plus more to taste
- 1 cup jasmine rice
- 3 quarts chicken stock (page 6)
- 1 (2- by 1-inch) piece fresh ginger, peeled and cut into ¼-inch-thick coins
- Freshly ground black pepper

Garnishes
- Finely chopped scallions, white and light green parts only
- Finely chopped fresh cilantro
- Coarsely chopped roasted peanuts
- Fried shallots (page 9)
- Chinese Doughnuts (optional; page 48), sliced

Serves 6

1.
Bring a large pot of water to a boil over high heat. Add the chicken, scallions, ginger, and salt and boil for 15 minutes, then turn off the heat, cover the pot, and let stand for 15 minutes. If your chicken is larger than 3 pounds, let stand 10 minutes longer.

2.
Just before the chicken is ready, prepare a large ice-water bath. When the chicken is done, remove it from the pot and immediately submerge it in the ice-water bath, which will stop the cooking and give the meat a firmer texture. Let stand 20 minutes until the chicken is cool enough to handle easily, then remove from the water and pat dry. Pull the chicken meat from the bones, discarding the bones and skin. Shred the meat with your fingers; you should have about 4 cups. Reserve 2 cups of the chicken cooking water and strain through a fine-mesh strainer; discard the remaining cooking liquid. Discard bones and skin and set meat aside. (This can be done a day ahead.)

3.
While the chicken is cooking, prepare the rice. Place the rice in a fine-mesh sieve and rinse well under cold running water. In a large pot, combine the rice, stock, ginger, and the 2 cups reserved chicken cooking water. Bring to a boil over high heat, lower the heat to a simmer, then cook, uncovered, for 1 hour. The rice will have broken down and the mixture will have a porridge-like consistency. Season to taste with salt.

4.
To ready the garnishes, put the scallions, cilantro, peanuts, fried shallots, and doughnut slices in separate small bowls. Ladle the porridge into warmed bowls. Top each serving with an equal amount of the chicken and a pinch of pepper. Pass the garnishes at the table.

Simple Fish Soup
—

I love this soup, and it's one I remember my mother making for the family when I was a kid. It's so simple and easy and cooks in only 20 minutes; no stock is required because you're using a whole fish—the bones for the broth, and the fillets for the finished soup— a good way to extract flavor from just a few ingredients. The fish head has lots of rich flavor, so make sure you add it to the pot. Even on a hot summer day, this soup is a great way to start a meal. This soup should be made with flavorful tomatoes; don't make it if your tomatoes taste like Styrofoam.

- 1 (1½- to 2-pound) whole branzino or black bass, cleaned
- 1 teaspoon fish sauce (see page 36)
- 1 teaspoon cornstarch
- 3 tablespoons vegetable oil
- 1 cup thinly sliced shallots (2 extra-large shallots)
- 1 teaspoon minced garlic
- 2 cups diced fresh or canned tomatoes
- 1 (2- by 1-inch) piece fresh ginger, cut into ¼-inch-thick coins
- 1 Thai chile, stemmed and sliced on the diagonal
- 2 teaspoons freshly squeezed lime juice
- ⅓ cup chopped fresh cilantro
- 1 tablespoon toasted garlic (see page 25)

Serves 6 as an appetizer

1.
Following the directions on page 23, fillet the fish. Alternatively, ask your fishmonger to fillet the fish for you, but make sure you keep the skeleton, including the head.

2.
Slice the fillets into 1-inch-wide strips and place them in a bowl. Add the fish sauce and cornstarch and toss to coat evenly. Chop the fish skeleton into thirds.

3.
In a large pot, heat the oil over medium-high heat. Add the shallots and cook, stirring occasionally, for about 5 minutes, until just softened. Add the garlic and cook for an additional 30 seconds. Add the tomatoes, ginger, chile, the fish skeleton and head, and 2 quarts water, increase the heat to high, and bring to a boil. Lower the heat to a steady simmer and simmer for 1 hour. Remove the fish skeleton and head and discard.

4.
Just before serving, add the fish strips and lime juice to the pot and simmer for 3 to 5 minutes, until the fish is opaque throughout. Taste the broth and adjust the seasoning with fish sauce.

5.
Ladle into warmed soup bowls and garnish with the cilantro and toasted garlic, dividing them evenly. Serve immediately.

How to Fillet a Whole Fish

To fillet a whole fish, first trim off the tail, then make a cut behind the head, angling the knife toward the front of the fish. Cut down to the bone. Next make a long cut along the backbone of the fish and run the knife blade under the fillet, cutting as close to the bones as possible. Release the fillet from the skeleton. Flip the fish over and repeat on the second side.

Hot and Sour Shrimp Soup

—

A version of this soup is made throughout Vietnam, though it probably originated in the south of the country, where tropical fruit and tamarind are abundant. The pineapple gives the soup sweetness while the tamarind lends tartness (vinegar or lime juice can also be used as a souring agent). *Bac ha* is the stem of the taro plant. It's a celery-like vegetable that stays crisp even when simmered in soup. It's fun to look for it in Asian grocery stores, but if you can't find it, don't worry—the soup will be just fine without it, though I sometimes add some shredded iceberg lettuce in its place.

- 2½ quarts chicken stock (see page 6)
- 2 ounces seedless tamarind pulp (see page 212)
- 2 Thai chiles, stemmed and halved lengthwise
- 2 tablespoons fish sauce (see page 36)
- 1 tablespoon plus 1 teaspoon freshly squeezed lime juice
- ¼ teaspoon kosher salt
- 8 ounces medium shrimp, peeled, deveined, and cut in half lengthwise
- ½ medium pineapple, peeled, cut lengthwise into 6 pieces, core trimmed away, and cut crosswise into ⅛-inch-thick slices (about 1½ cups)
- 3 cups mung bean sprouts (see page 207)
- 1½ cups *bac ha*, peeled and cut into ⅛-inch-thick rounds, or shredded iceberg lettuce (optional)
- 2 tablespoons chopped fresh cilantro
- 1 tablespoon toasted garlic (below)

Serves 6 as an appetizer

1.
In a large pot, combine the stock, tamarind pulp, and chiles and bring to a boil over high heat. Lower the heat to a steady simmer and simmer for 15 minutes, stirring occasionally with a whisk to break up the tamarind pulp. Remove from the heat, strain through a fine-mesh sieve, and discard the solids. Return the liquid to the pot.

2.
Stir in the fish sauce, lime juice, and salt and bring to a simmer over medium heat. Add the shrimp and pineapple and cook for about 30 seconds, until the shrimp just turn pink.

3.
Divide the bean sprouts and *bac ha* among warmed soup bowls. Ladle the hot soup into the bowls and garnish with the cilantro and toasted garlic, dividing them evenly. Serve immediately.

Toasted Garlic

—

This is a frequently used garnish on rice dishes, soups, and salads. Toasting garlic gently makes it crunchy and sweet. Note that this is a recipe for toasted garlic, not burned garlic, so be sure to pay attention when you are frying it, as it can darken quickly. You can double the recipe, but if you want to make more than that, it's best to do it in two (or more) batches.

- ¼ cup plus 2 tablespoons vegetable oil
- 2 tablespoons finely chopped garlic

Makes 2 tablespoons

In a small saucepan, heat the oil over medium-low heat. Add the garlic and cook, stirring frequently to prevent burning, for about 5 minutes, until the garlic is light golden brown. Don't overcook the garlic or it will become acrid. Pour into a fine-mesh sieve, reserving the oil, and transfer the garlic to paper towels to drain. Save the oil (it's great on rice or in salad dressing); it will keep in a tightly covered container for up to 1 week. Use the toasted garlic the same day as it's made.

Crab and Corn Soup

—

Some Vietnamese dishes clearly demonstrate the influence that the French had on local food. This soup is one of them. Although crab is eaten all over Vietnam (mostly freshwater crabs), corn wasn't eaten in Vietnam until the French introduced it. This soup demonstrates the intermingling of the two food cultures: using an ingredient common in Vietnam, the crab, but presenting it in a European way, as a light first-course soup rather than a meal-in-a-bowl noodle soup. You can use any kind of crab here. In our restaurants, we use Dungeness, which is plentiful and locally caught. This soup is quick to make, particularly if you buy cooked crabmeat.

- 3 quarts chicken stock (see page 6)
- 2½ cups fresh corn kernels, coarsely chopped, with cobs reserved (from about 2 ears corn)
- 12 ounces fresh-cooked crabmeat (from about two 2-pound Dungeness crabs), picked over for shell bits
- Kosher salt
- Toasted sesame oil, for garnish
- Ground white pepper, for garnish
- ⅓ cup chopped scallions, white and light green parts only, for garnish

Serves 6 as an appetizer

1.
In a large pot, combine the stock and corncobs and bring to a boil over high heat. Lower the heat to a simmer and cook for 20 minutes. Remove and discard corncobs.

2.
Stir in the crabmeat and corn kernels and simmer for 10 minutes, until the corn is tender. Season to taste with salt.

3.
Ladle the soup into warmed soup bowls and garnish each serving with a few drops of sesame oil, a pinch of white pepper, and some of the scallions. Serve immediately.

Variation: Crab and Asparagus Soup
In spring, asparagus replaces the corn in this soup. Asparagus was first planted in Vietnam by the French, and both fresh green and canned white asparagus are still popular there today. Substitute 1 large bunch asparagus for the corn. Snap off the ends of the stalks where they naturally break, and add the ends to the chicken stock in place of the corncobs, then simmer and discard as directed. Slice the stalks on the diagonal into ½-inch-thick pieces and add to the pot in place of the corn kernels. Simmer for 6 to 8 minutes, until the asparagus is tender, then ladle into warmed bowls and garnish as directed.

Street Food

When I was a kid, a cook would set up a green canvas army tent behind my family's general store in Đà Lat. He made only one dish: crispy egg noodles with seafood. I would go there frequently after school (we lived over the store) while I was waiting for my parents to finish work. I'd sit on a low stool waiting for my order, listening to the sizzle of liquid hitting the hot wok and the monsoon rains battering the tent, the air thick with the smell of browning noodles. It's one of my first food memories.

Vietnam is full of snackers who are never far from a quick bite. Because the country is lacking in entry-level jobs, and because there is a huge market for food cooked outside the home (most home kitchens are poorly equipped or very cramped), people start their own ad hoc businesses, including food stalls. The entrepreneurial spirit drives cooks to the streets, where they master the art of making a single dish: sticky rice, banana fritters, green papaya salad. The cooks employ every technique—deep-frying in jury-rigged pots set over open fires, stir-frying in big woks over high flames, steaming in giant lidded bamboo baskets balanced atop rickety propane

burners—to make snacks that are served and eaten on the spot. Even talented home cooks don't make these dishes at home. Yes, space is at a premium, but an attitude persists too: why try to make something at home that you can so easily and cheaply purchase from someone who has perfected the recipe? Since we don't have the luxury of a steamed-bun vendor or *bánh mì* stand on every corner here in the United States, making these snacks at home is the only option.

Unlike the subsequent chapters in this book, which explain a single technique, the unifying element of the recipes in this chapter is that they're some of the most popular foods that you'll find sold from stalls in cities and small towns throughout Vietnam.

Street food offers a direct connection between the cook and the eater. Part of what makes the food so appealing is that it's superfresh. You're literally watching the dishes being made, start to finish, in front of your eyes. It is Vietnam's answer to fast food, only it is far more interesting, varied, and well prepared.

Unlike a full-service restaurant, street vendors usually make only one or two items. That means they've spent their entire careers perfecting their recipe, customizing their equipment, sourcing the best ingredients. After trying an excellent bite from a vendor, I've often asked for the recipe. Not a single cook has ever given me one. The recipe, and the practiced technique, is as much a commodity as the food they're selling you.

The three common denominators that help identify the best vendors: they're usually stationary, serve a single dish or one ingredient prepared in a few different ways, and they're always crowded.

In Vietnam, the foods you buy from street vendors aren't categorized as hors d'oeuvres, appetizers, or main courses, though some items are traditionally served at certain times of the day. Rice porridge (page 20) and soup are found in the morning and are rarely eaten after lunch. Sweets stalls might open for only a few hours each evening. A soup vendor might pop up for a few hours during the morning commute, then pack up until the next day. We serve many of the recipes in this chapter at The Slanted Door, where they're some of the most popular items on the menu. Those favored Vietnamese street foods inspired the first dishes we served when we opened in 1995, and they

have remained on the menu ever since. Some, like the fresh spring rolls (page 44), are easy. Others, like the filled rice-paper packets called *Bánh Cuốn* (page 62), require some practice to perfect. As the Vietnamese vendors know well, mastery comes only from repetition. I think you'll find the flavors so compelling that the labor will be worth it. Once you get the

hang of a few of these recipes, you'll probably find yourself making them a lot. Without the chaos, the heat, and the noise, it'll never be exactly like eating on the streets of Vietnam, but the food will still be delicious.

Green Papaya Salad with Rau Ram, Peanuts, and Crispy Shallots

—

Almost every country in Southeast Asia has a version of this salad. It's so common in Vietnam that you can buy all of the ingredients for it, prepped and ready to toss together at home, at the market: shredded green (unripe) papaya, small plastic bags of dressing, and fried shallots.

Unlike ripe papaya, which has soft orange flesh and black seeds, the flesh of a green papaya is pale green and firm and the seeds are white. In Vietnam, the papayas are usually hacked into small, irregular strips with a sharp knife, which gives the salad a nice texture. At the restaurants, we julienne the papaya with a mandoline because it's faster and easier. The addition of fried tofu, celery, and cucumber aren't traditional, but I like the flavor and texture they add. *Rau ram* is a common Vietnamese green herb with a flavor somewhere between cilantro and mint. If you can't find it, a mixture of spearmint and cilantro is a fine substitute.

The salad is especially good topped with shredded Beef Jerky (page 37).

- 2 cups canola oil
- 6 ounces medium-firm tofu, patted dry and cut into 3- by 3-inch squares, ¼ inch thick
- 1 large green papaya (about 2 pounds), peeled, halved, seeded, and finely julienned with a mandoline or sharp knife (about 5 cups shredded)
- ½ cup coarsely chopped fresh *rau ram* (see page 210) or a mixture of spearmint and cilantro
- ½ English cucumber, halved lengthwise and thinly sliced crosswise into half moons (about 1 cup)
- 2 celery stalks, thinly sliced
- ½ cup pickled carrots (see page 35)
- ¾ cup flavored fish sauce (see page 35)
- 2 tablespoons shallot oil (see page 9) or canola oil
- ¼ cup roasted peanuts, finely chopped, for garnish
- ⅓ cup fried shallots (see page 9), for garnish

Serves 6

1.
In an 8-inch frying pan, heat the canola oil over high heat to 350°F on a deep-frying thermometer. When the oil is ready, carefully add the tofu slices and fry, turning once, for 15 minutes, until golden brown on both sides. Using a slotted spoon, transfer the tofu to paper towels to drain. When cool, cut into into strips ¼ inch wide.

2.
In a large bowl, combine the papaya, *rau ram*, cucumber, celery, carrot, and tofu strips. Pour the flavored fish sauce and shallot oil over the top and toss to coat evenly. Transfer to a serving platter and garnish with the peanuts and shallots. Serve immediately.

Pickled Carrots

—

These quick pickles are the perfect foil for rich foods. They are often served alongside fried things and are always piled on top of meat-filled bánh mì sandwiches. If you like, use julienned daikon (see page 204) in addition to carrots.

- ¼ cup distilled white vinegar
- ¼ cup sugar
- ¼ teaspoon kosher salt
- ½ cup peeled and finely julienned carrots

Makes ½ cup

In a small bowl, combine the vinegar, sugar, and salt and stir until the sugar and salt have dissolved. Add the carrots and let stand for at least 20 minutes before serving. If not using right away, cover and refrigerate for up to a week. Drain the carrots well before before using.

Flavored Fish Sauce

—

On its own, fish sauce is an assertive condiment. But blended with water, sugar, and an acidic element, it becomes a mellow dipping sauce, despite the addition of chiles and garlic. This sauce is frequently served alongside fried items and is also used as a salad dressing.

- ½ cup fish sauce (see page 36)
- ⅓ cup sugar
- ¼ cup distilled white vinegar or freshly squeezed lemon juice
- 2 cloves garlic, minced
- 1 to 2 Thai chiles, stemmed and minced

Makes 1½ cups

In a small bowl, combine the fish sauce, sugar, vinegar or lemon juice, and ½ cup water and stir until the sugar has dissolved. Add the garlic and chiles and stir to combine. Use immediately, or refrigerate for up to 1 week if made with vinegar or up to 2 days if made with lemon juice.

Fish Sauce
—

Fish sauce is one of the most widely used condiments in Southeast Asia. It's used as a base for dipping sauces, in salad dressings, to add salt and savory flavor to cooked dishes and drizzled on finished dishes.

It is the liquid extracted from fish—usually anchovies—that accumulates following salting and then prolonged fermentation. To make first-grade fish sauce, freshly caught fish are rinsed and layered with sea salt (usually two to three parts fish to one part salt by weight) in large earthenware jars or wooden barrels. A bamboo mat is placed just inside the rim of the vessel and topped with a weight so the fish don't float to the surface. The vessels are then left in the sun for between nine months and one year.

The containers are periodically uncovered to expose the contents to direct, hot sunshine, and over time the liquid takes on an amber color and a complex flavor. After the fish have fermented for the required time, a spigot at the bottom of the vessel is opened and the liquid is drained off through the settled fish remains. The liquid is strained into clean jars and left to sit in the sun for a few more weeks. To make second- and third-grade sauces, salt water is added to the fermented fish sediment and left to sit for another two to three months. These lower grades lack the pure flavor and complexity of the first-grade sauce. Sugar and caramel color are typically added to make up for what is not occurring naturally.

Not all bottles of fish sauce are well labeled, but if you can find it, buy one that lists only fish and salt as ingredients. The sauce should be clear, the color of iced tea, and free of sediment.

When I call for fish sauce in my recipes, it's the first-grade stuff, called *nuoc mam cot* or *nuoc mam nhi* that I'm talking about. Two recipes in the book, Halibut Vermicelli on page 56 and the Beer-Battered Soft-Shell Crab on page 199, call for anchovy fish sauce, or *mam nem*. This fermented anchovy dipping sauce is made from whole anchovies that have been ground up. It is basically an unstrained version of *nuoc mam*, with a much more pungent and assertive flavor.

Beef Jerky

—

In the States, jerky is a snack that people buy at gas stations and eat on the road. In Vietnam, the sweet, spicy beef is usually used as a condiment, finely shredded and scattered atop salads as a garnish, like the green papaya salad on page 34. What makes Vietnamese (and Chinese) jerky different from what you find in the states is the marinade, which is typically wetter and contains more sugar. Asian beef jerky is also often unsmoked. Be sure to cut the beef into slices with the grain. If you cut it against the grain, it will break apart into tiny pieces when cooked. To make it easier to slice the meat thinly, let it cool completely after cooking.

- 2 cups light soy sauce (see page 215)
- 8 scallions, trimmed and cut into 3-inch lengths
- 2 pounds beef top round
- 3 tablespoons honey
- 1 tablespoon plus 1 teaspoon roasted chile paste (see page 117)
- 1 tablespoon plus 1 teaspoon fish sauce (see page 36)
- 3 teaspoons minced garlic
- 1 teaspoon red pepper flakes
- 1 teaspoon minced Thai chile
- Kosher salt
- 3 tablespoons canola oil

Makes about 4 cups

1.
In a large pot, combine 1½ cups of the soy sauce, the scallions, and 8 cups water. Add the beef and bring to a boil over high heat. Lower the heat to a simmer and cook, uncovered, for 1¼ hours. Remove pot from heat and remove the beef from the liquid. Discard the liquid and let the beef cool to room temperature.

2.
To make the cooking liquid, in a large bowl combine 1 cup water, the remaining ½ cup soy sauce, the honey, chile paste, fish sauce, 2 teaspoons of the garlic, the red pepper flakes, Thai chile, and salt. Whisk to combine.

3.
When the beef is cool, thinly slice the meat with the grain into ⅛-inch-thick slices. Add the slices to the cooking liquid and toss to coat.

4.
In a large sauté pan, heat the oil over medium heat. Add the remaining 1 teaspoon garlic and cook, stirring, for 15 seconds, until aromatic. Pour the beef and its marinade into the pan, decrease the heat to medium-low, and cook, stirring occasionally, until the liquid has completely reduced and the beef is glazed with the marinade.

5.
Set a wire rack on a rimmed baking sheet. Arrange the beef slices on the rack in a single layer. Let cool to room temperature. The finished texture will be moister than American beef jerky, but still chewy. The jerky will keep, tightly wrapped and refrigerated, for 4 days.

Pork and Shrimp Spring Rolls

—

When I first decided to open a restaurant, I had never cooked professionally. My family maxed out sixteen credit cards to buy a small space on Valencia Street in San Francisco's Mission District, a leap of faith based entirely on my hunch that the simple dishes of Vietnam—dishes that my mother made at home—would be popular in San Francisco, especially if they were presented in a beautiful space and made with good-quality ingredients.

It was Mom's spring rolls specifically that made me want to open a restaurant. I just knew they were something that American diners would love. Every Vietnamese restaurant makes a version of these rice-paper rolls, filled with everything from pork to tofu to fish. But my mother's version has an unusual twist. She had worked as a nurse in a French hospital in Vietnam, where she learned to make mayonnaise using the oil left over from frying shallots. She came up with the idea of adding a smear of mayonnaise to the spring rolls to moisten them—an addition you won't see in any other recipe. If you don't have shallot oil, you can make the mayonnaise with canola oil. However, the homemade mayonnaise is crucial, and you should omit it rather than use store-bought mayonnaise.

We sell about eight hundred thousand spring rolls every year at The Slanted Door, most of which are rolled by Mrs. Tran, who has worked at the restaurant since the beginning. A few years ago, I shared the recipe for our spring rolls with *The New York Times*, and my mother was sure the restaurant was going to go out of business, because I'd given away the family jewel.

For best results, roll the spring rolls on a plastic or wooden cutting board; the rice paper tends to stick to stone surfaces. And pay attention to the size of the rolls—you are not making cigars or burritos. When you roll, pull the rice paper tight to form a compact cylinder. And when you cut the rolls, don't cut them on the diagonal, which will cause the filling to fall out.

- 10 ounces dried rice vermicelli (see page 12)
- 15 medium-size shrimp, peeled and deveined
- 8 ounces boneless pork shoulder
- 1 egg yolk
- ½ cup shallot oil (see page 9) or canola oil
- ¼ teaspoon kosher salt
- 30 fresh mint leaves
- 1 head red leaf lettuce, leaves separated
- 10 (12-inch) rice-paper rounds
- Peanut sauce (see page 47), for serving

Makes 10 rolls, enough to serve 10 people as an appetizer

1.
Bring a saucepan filled with water to a boil over high heat. Add the rice vermicelli and cook until they are tender yet still have some bite, according to package directions. Drain the noodles, rinse them under cold running water until cool, then rinse under very hot running water before rinsing them a second time under cold running water. This cold-hot-cold rinse prevents the noodles from sticking together and breaking. Set the noodles aside.

2.
Refill the saucepan with water and bring to a boil over high heat. Add the shrimp and cook for about 3 minutes, until bright pink. Using a slotted spoon, transfer the shrimp to a colander and rinse under cold running water. Transfer to paper towels to drain. Cut each shrimp in half lengthwise and set aside.

3.
Return the water to a boil and add the pork. Decrease the heat so the water is at a simmer and cook for 20 minutes, until the meat is cooked through. Transfer to a plate and poke it with a chopstick; the juices should run clear. Let cool completely, then cut against the grain into ⅛-inch-thick slices. (The meat can be cooked a day ahead, covered, and refrigerated. Slice just before using.)

4.
To make the shallot mayonnaise, put the egg yolk in a bowl, and set the bowl on top of a dry kitchen towel. Pour the shallot oil into a measuring cup. Whisk the yolk well, then begin adding the oil, one droplet at a time at first, until the mixture thickens. Continue to add the oil, drop by drop and whisking constantly, until the mixture is well emulsified and thick. Add the remaining oil in a steady stream, whisking constantly, until all of it has been incorporated. The mayonnaise will be very thick. Whisk in the salt and set aside.

5.
Put the shrimp, pork, lettuce, mint, and mayonnaise within easy reach of your work surface. Fill a large bowl with very hot water. Working with 1 rice-paper round at a time, dip it into the hot water until pliable. This will take only about

Continued →

5 seconds. Remove the round from the water and spread it flat on the work surface.

6.
Lay 1 lettuce leaf over the bottom one-third of the rice-paper round, flattening it to crack the rib. Spread a generous teaspoon of the mayonnaise over the lettuce, then top with 3 mint leaves, arranged end to end, and a few slices of pork. Top with about ½ cup of the noodles.

7.
Fold in the left and right sides of the rice paper, then lift the bottom edge up and over the filling. Tightly roll the rice paper away from you one turn, enclosing the filling completely. Arrange 3 pieces of shrimp, cut side up and end to end, in a row on the rice paper, then roll another turn to enclose the shrimp. Continue rolling as tightly as possible, tucking in the sides, until you have formed a compact cylinder. Place the roll on a platter or baking sheet and cover with a damp kitchen towel to keep moist. Repeat with the remaining rice paper and filling ingredients. The rolls can be made up to 2 hours in advance. Refrigerate them, covered with the damp towel, until serving.

8.
Just before serving, cut each roll crosswise into thirds and arrange on a platter. Serve the peanut sauce in small bowls for dipping.

Peanut Sauce

—

In the late 1970s shortly after my family moved to San Francisco from a refugee camp in Guam, my mother took a job in a sewing shop. She rode the bus back and forth to work, from our house in Chinatown to the Mission District. While she and the other women waited for the bus, they swapped recipes. One of the recipes she picked up was this version of peanut sauce.

There are a lot of recipes for peanut sauce out there—some with coconut milk, some with curry—but this one is different from most. It contains cooked sweet (glutinous) rice, which gives the sauce a velvety texture, and red miso, which gives it a richer, more savory flavor. No one can ever guess the ingredients, and after fifteen years of making this peanut sauce at the restaurant, I'm still not tired of eating it.

- 1 cup sweet (glutinous) rice (see page 211)
- ½ cup roasted peanuts
- 2 cloves garlic
- 1 Thai chile, stemmed
- 3 tablespoons red miso
- 3 tablespoons ketchup
- 3 tablespoons canola oil
- 3 tablespoons sugar
- 2 tablespoons vegetarian stir-fry sauce (see page 215)
- 1½ teaspoons freshly squeezed lemon juice
- ¼ teaspoon toasted sesame oil

Makes about 2 cups

1.
Rinse the rice in a fine-mesh sieve until the water runs clear, then transfer to a heavy-bottomed pot with a lid. Add 2 cups water and bring to a boil over high heat. Decrease the heat to low, cover, and cook for about 15 minutes, until the water is absorbed and the rice is tender. Remove from the heat and let stand, covered, for 10 minutes. Then uncover, fluff with a fork, and let cool to room temperature. Alteratively, the rice can be prepared in a rice cooker.

2.
In a food processor, combine the cooled rice, peanuts, garlic, chile, miso, ketchup, canola oil, sugar, stir-fry sauce, lemon juice, and sesame oil and process until the mixture is a fine paste. Thin with water (about ¼ cup) until the texture is smooth and creamy. Transfer to a bowl, cover, and refrigerate until ready to serve. The sauce will keep, refrigerated, for up to 4 days.

Chinese Doughnuts

—

These batons of crisp dough, more savory than sweet, are fried on the streets of Vietnam (and elsewhere in Asia, including China and Thailand), then piled high in bamboo baskets and sold to passersby. Both in Vietnam and the States, they're typically eaten for breakfast, dunked into mugs of warm soy milk or sliced and used as a garnish for rice porridge (page 20). The dough has to rest for at least 8 hours before the doughnuts are fried, so plan accordingly.

- 3 cups all-purpose flour, plus more for dusting work surface
- 2 tablespoons baking powder
- ¼ teaspoon baking soda
- 1 tablespoon sugar
- ½ teaspoon kosher salt
- 1 egg yolk
- 2 tablespoons canola oil, plus more for deep-frying

Makes 6 doughnuts

1.
In a large bowl, combine the flour, baking powder, and baking soda and mix until well-combined. Set aside.

2.
In a separate small bowl, dissolve the sugar and salt in 1 cup hot water.

3.
Make a well in the center of the dry ingredients and add the egg yolk. Gradually pour the water mixture into the well, whisking to combine with the yolk. Switch to a wooden spoon and continue mixing until the wet and dry ingredients are well combined. The dough will be sticky; if it looks dry, add more water by the tablespoonful. Drizzle in the 2 tablespoons canola oil and knead into the dough. Cover the bowl with plastic wrap and let rest at room temperature, then refrigerate overnight.

4.
Flour a work surface and your hands. Divide the dough into thirds and transfer one-third to your work surface. Roll out the dough into a 6-inch by 12-inch rectangle about ½ inch thick. Cut into twelve 1½-inch-wide strips, and gently score the center of each strip with a sharp knife (do not cut all the way through). Lightly brush the tops of 2 strips with water, then stack the other 2 strips on top, scored sides facing to form doubled stacks. Gently press the top strip on each stack so it adheres to the bottom strip. Let rest for 15 minutes. Repeat with the remaining dough. You should have 6 doubled stacks, or doughnuts.

5.
Pour the oil to a depth of 2 inches into a wok or large, high-sided pot and heat to 350°F on a deep-frying thermometer. When the oil is ready, carefully add 3 doughnuts and cook, turning them continuously and submerging them beneath the oil, for 4 to 6 minutes, until golden brown. Using a spider or tongs, transfer the doughnuts to paper towels to drain. Repeat with the remaining 3 doughnuts, allowing the oil to return to temperature before adding them. Serve the doughnuts warm.

Bánh Mì

—

In the last couple of years, *bánh mì*, a baguette sandwich that has been a favorite snack in Vietnam since French colonial days, has become popular in the States. The sandwiches are sold almost everywhere in Vietnam, filled with almost anything. Although I've tried many, many versions of *bánh mì* in the States, none has been quite as good as what I can get back in Vietnam. Happily, a very good version can be made at home.

Best bread:

This might be the most important element of a *bánh mì*. In Vietnam, the baguettes are made with a combination of rice flour and wheat flour. They have a crackly exterior and a fluffy interior. The crust shouldn't be too robust, though, or the sandwich will be difficult to chew and you'll tear up the roof of your mouth. This is a case when you don't want to use the fanciest artisanal country loaf or the crustiest baguette. A toasted supermarket baguette, a bolillo (a torpedo-shaped Mexican roll), or a roll that you find in an Asian market is your best bet. Split the roll lengthwise and pull out most of the bread guts. This will ensure that your sandwich isn't too doughy and that you can get your mouth around it.

Filling:

Dozens of different fillings for these sandwiches are possible: headcheese, Vietnamese bologna, grilled meat (chicken, pork, or beef), or even vegetarian versions with tofu or mushrooms. My favorite fillings are Lemongrass Pork (page 55) and Mama's Meatballs (page 52), which makes a saucy, messy, Sloppy Joe–like sandwich.

Toppings:

A *bánh mì* needs pickled carrots (page 35), thin slices of jalapeño chile, cucumber, and lots of fresh cilantro. These toppings give the sandwich flavor and offset the fattiness of the fillings. Without these additions, you'll still have a tasty sandwich, but it won't be a *bánh mì*. Two more tips: spread both cut sides of each roll with a little mayonnaise to ensure the sandwich isn't dry, and finish it with a drizzle of Golden Mountain or Maggi seasoning sauce (page 214).

Mama's Meatballs

—

The recipe for these meatballs comes from my aunt, who we all call Mama. In the Vietnamese kitchen, meatballs are all about texture: fish balls must be as springy as rubber balls, and pork meatballs, like these, must fall apart in a sandwich, approximating an American Sloppy Joe. I like to hand-chop the pork for meatballs, starting with fatty pork shoulder. If you choose to have your butcher grind the meat, ask for a coarse grind. These meatballs make a wonderful, messy sandwich, but they're also good spooned over steamed rice. This recipe yields a lot of meatballs. But I figure if you're going to go to the trouble of making them, you may as well make a big batch. If you aren't feeding a crowd, they freeze well.

Sauce
- 1 pound boneless pork shoulder, finely hand-chopped (see below), or coarsely ground pork shoulder
- 4 cups chicken stock (see page 6) or water
- ¾ cup canola oil
- ¼ cup minced garlic
- 1 tablespoon red pepper flakes
- 1½ teaspoons ground annatto seeds (see page 202)
- 2 cups finely chopped shallots (about 5 large shallots)
- 2 cups finely diced yellow onions
- 1 cup vegetarian stir-fry sauce (see page 215)
- 1 cup ketchup
- 1½ tablespoons light soy sauce (see page 215)

Meatballs
- 3 pounds boneless pork shoulder, finely hand-chopped (see below), or coarsely ground
- 1½ cups finely diced fresh water chestnuts (see page 213) or jicama (see page 206)
- 1 cup diced yellow onion
- 1 cup finely diced shallots
- ½ cup chopped scallions, white and light green parts only
- ⅓ cup fried shallots (see page 9), coarsely chopped
- ¼ cup chopped fresh cilantro
- 2 teaspoons kosher salt
- 2 teaspoons freshly ground black pepper
- 2 tablespoons light soy sauce (see page 215)

Makes about 48 2-inch meatballs

How to Hand-Chop Pork

1.
Trim the pork shoulder of some but not all of the fat.

2.
Cut the pork into ¼-inch slices, then cut each slice into ¼-inch ribbons, then cut the ribbons crosswise into small cubes.

3.
With a cleaver or heavy chef's knife, finely chop the cubes, running the knife through the meat until it's evenly chopped but still more coarsely textured than store bought preground pork.

1.

To make the sauce, in a large, wide, high-sided pot, combine the pork and 2 cups of the stock and bring to a boil over high heat. Decrease the heat so the liquid is at a steady simmer and simmer for 15 minutes, skimming any scum that forms on the surface. Remove from the heat, let cool slightly, and transfer the mixture to a blender or food processor. Process until smooth. Set aside.

2.

Return the empty pot to the stove top, add the oil, and heat over medium heat. Add the garlic and cook, stirring occasionally, for 2 minutes, until lightly toasted. Add the red pepper flakes and annatto and cook, stirring, for 30 seconds more. Add the shallots and onions and cook, stirring, for about 5 minutes, until softened.

Add the stir-fry sauce, ketchup, and soy sauce and stir to combine. Pour in the pureed pork mixture and the remaining 2 cups stock and mix well.

3.

Increase the heat to high and bring the mixture to a boil, then decrease the heat until the liquid is at a steady simmer. Cook, stirring occasionally, for 15 minutes.

4.

While the sauce is simmering, make the meatballs. In a large bowl, combine all of the ingredients. Using your hands, gently but thoroughly mix the ingredients together. Take care not to overwork the mixture or the meatballs will be tough. Form the mixture into loosely packed balls about 2 inches in diameter.

Add the meatballs to the simmering sauce. The meatballs can be crowded in the pan but they should all be below the surface of the sauce. Cook, without stirring, for 45 minutes, until they are cooked through. Do not let the liquid boil, or the meatballs will break apart. To test if the meatballs are ready, retrieve a meatball and cut it open; it should no longer be pink in the center.

5.

Remove from the heat and serve right away. Or, if you're making the meatballs in advance, let cool and then reheat them fully in the sauce before serving. Cooling them in the sauce will prevent them from drying out.

Note: To Freeze

The meatballs can be frozen: Put them in a single layer on a baking sheet and transfer to the freezer. When completely frozen, transfer the meatballs to a resealable plastic bag and freeze until ready to use. They can be added to the sauce while still frozen; increase the cooking time by 10 minutes. The cooked meatballs can also be frozen with the sauce. Let the cooked meatballs and sauce cool, then transfer meatballs and sauce to a resealable plastic container, filling the container three-quarters full. Cover and freeze. Meatballs (and meatballs and sauce) will keep, frozen, for up to 3 months.

Lemongrass Pork

—

This cheater's version of porchetta makes a great filling for *bánh mì* (page 51), though it's also good on its own, with rice and a vegetable side dish.

- ¾ cup finely chopped lemongrass (see page 207)
- ¼ cup chopped garlic
- 3 tablespoons kosher salt
- 1½ tablespoons coriander seeds, toasted in a dry pan until fragrant, cooled, and ground
- 1½ tablespoons freshly ground black pepper
- ¼ cup canola oil
- 4 pounds boneless pork loin

Serves 6 as a main course or makes enough meat for 8 to 10 sandwiches

1.
In a bowl, combine the lemongrass, garlic, salt, coriander, and pepper and stir to mix. Add the oil and stir until a thick paste forms. Set aside.

2.
Place the pork loin on a cutting board. Beginning at one end of the loin, make a horizontal cut about 1-inch deep. Continue cutting the length of the loin. Then, return to the start of the cut and deepen the cut, pulling back the meat as you go, until the pork loin opens like a magazine. Do not cut all the way through.

3.
Spread three-quarters of the spice mixture on the top of the pork and then roll the pork into a tight cylinder, securing it at 3-inch intervals with butcher's twine. Rub the remaining mixture on the outside of the meat. Place the meat on a rimmed baking sheet, cover loosely with plastic wrap, and refrigerate for at least 8 hours.

4.
When you are ready to cook the meat, remove it from the refrigerator and bring it to room temperature. Preheat the oven to 325°F.

5.
Roast the pork for about 1¼ hours, until an instant-read thermometer inserted into the thickest part of the shoulder registers 140°F. Transfer the shoulder to a platter and tent with aluminum foil.

6.
If serving the pork hot as a main course, let rest for about 30 minutes then slice the shoulder and serve. If you're planning to use the pork for sandwiches, let cool completely before slicing.

Halibut Vermicelli with Dill and Pineapple-Anchovy Sauce

—

When I returned to Vietnam in 1992, one of the first places I went was *Cha Cá La Vong*, a restaurant in Hanoi that has been in business for more than one hundred years. The restaurant only makes one thing: fried fish that has been marinated in turmeric, cooked with dill (an herb widely used in northern Vietnam) and scallions, and served with a pineapple-anchovy sauce. At the restaurant, you finish the cooking at your table, dipping the fish in hot oil.

In Vietnam, pineapple and anchovy are often combined to make a pungent condiment that is equal parts sweet and salty. The anchovy fish sauce used in this recipe is known as *mam nem* and is different from the more commonly used fish sauce called *nuoc mam*. This thicker sauce, cloudy and gray with sediment, is too strong to eat on its own, but is really good when blended with pineapple.

Pineapple-Anchovy Sauce
- ¼ cup anchovy fish sauce (see page 36)
- 1 cup diced fresh pineapple
- 1 clove garlic, smashed
- 1 Thai chile, stemmed
- 1 tablespoon plus 1 teaspoon freshly squeezed lime juice
- 1 tablespoon sugar

- 2 pounds skinless halibut or other firm white fish fillets (such as cod or sea bass)
- 1 (16-ounce) package dried rice vermicelli (see page 13) or 3 pounds fresh rice noodles (see page 172)
- 1 cup vegetable oil
- ¼ cup fish sauce (see page 36)
- ½ teaspoon ground turmeric
- 1½ cups 2-inch-long scallion batons, white and light green parts only
- 1 cup fresh dill fronds
- ¼ cup chopped roasted peanuts, for garnish

Serves 6 as a main course

1.
To make the sauce, in a blender, combine the anchovy sauce, pineapple, garlic, chile, lime juice, and sugar and process until smooth. Taste and adjust the seasoning, adding more chile, sugar, and/or lime juice, if needed. The sauce should have the consistency of a thin fruit smoothie. Set aside.

2.
Arrange the halibut fillets lengthwise on a cutting board. Holding a sharp knife at a 45-degree angle, cut the fish cross-wise into slices about 1¼ inches thick. Set aside.

3.
If using dried vermicelli, bring a large pot filled with water to a boil over high heat. Add the rice vermicelli and cook until they are tender yet still have some bite, according to package directions. Drain the noodles, rinse them under cold running water until cool, then rinse under very hot running water before rinsing them a second time under cold running water. This cold-hot-cold rinse prevents the noodles from sticking together and breaking. Set the noodles aside.

4.
In a bowl, whisk together the oil, fish sauce, and turmeric. Add the fish and toss to coat evenly. Let marinate for at least 5 minutes but no more than 10 minutes. Meanwhile, finely julienne the scallion batons and place in a bowl. Add the dill and toss to mix. Divide the rice noodles among 6 serving plates and top each serving with 2 tablespoons of the pineapple-anchovy sauce.

5.
Heat a large nonstick sauté pan over high heat. When the pan is very hot, add half of the fish and marinade, arranging the pieces in a single layer. Cook for about 2 minutes, until very lightly browned. Using a fish spatula, carefully turn the fish pieces over and cook for about 1 minute on the second side. Add half of the dill-scallion mixture and sauté with the fish for about 20 seconds, just until the greens are wilted.

6.
Divide the fish and greens evenly among 3 of the serving plates, spooning them on top of the noodles and then drizzling each with some of the liquid from the pan.

7.
Wipe the sauté pan clean and repeat steps 5 and 6 with the remaining fish and marinade and dill-scallion mixture. Garnish each plate with some of the peanuts and serve immediately. Pass the remaining anchovy-pineapple sauce on the side.

Bánh Xèo: Crepe with Pork and Shrimp

—

The literal translation of *bánh xèo* is "sizzling cake," an apt description for this crispy crepe stuffed with bean sprouts, pork, and shrimp. The cooking technique will be familiar to anyone who has ever tried to make a French-style crepe, but the batter itself is different: it is eggless, made mostly from rice flour and dried mung beans, and is seasoned with turmeric and coconut milk. Because you can cook only one crepe at a time, plan to have some side dishes made before you get started, and then crank out the crepes, short-order-cook style. A nonstick pan or well-seasoned wok is essential to the success of this recipe; if you use a regular pan, the batter will stick like glue. Be sure to eat with lettuce and herbs.

Crepe Batter
- 1 cup rice flour (see page 210)
- ½ cup cornstarch
- ¼ teaspoon ground turmeric
- ¼ cup coconut milk
- 1 teaspoon kosher salt
- ½ cup thinly sliced scallion tops, dark green part only (cut into ¼-inch-thick slices)

Filling
- 6 to 9 tablespoons canola oil
- 8 ounces boneless lean pork shoulder, cut into 1 by 2 by ⅛-inch slices
- ½ small yellow onion, cut into ¼-inch-thick slices
- 6 medium-size shrimp, peeled, deveined, and halved lengthwise
- 2¼ cups mung bean sprouts (see page 207)

For Serving
- 24 red leaf lettuce leaves
- 6 large spearmint sprigs
- Flavored fish sauce (see page 35)

Makes 3 crepes; serves 6

1.
To make the crepe batter, in a bowl, stir together rice flour, cornstarch, and turmeric. Pour in the coconut milk, 2 cups water, and the salt and whisk until well combined. Let the batter sit for 10 minutes, then stir in the scallions. (The batter can be prepared up to 12 hours in advance, covered, and refrigerated. Stir in scallions just before using.)

2.
In a 10-inch nonstick frying pan, heat 1 tablespoon of the oil over high heat. When the oil is shimmering but not smoking, add one-third of the pork slices and cook, turning once, for about 3 minutes, until golden brown on both sides. Add one-third of the sliced onions and cook without stirring for 30 seconds more.

3.
Stir the batter well, then pour ⅓ cup into the hot pan over the pork and onions. Lift the pan and swirl it gently so the batter coats the entire bottom and halfway up the sides of the pan. Return the pan to the heat and cook the crepe for 1 minute, just until the batter takes on a dry appearance.

4.
Place 4 pieces of shrimp and ¾ cup bean sprouts on one-half of the crepe, cover the pan, and reduce the heat to medium. Cook for about 2 minutes, just until the edges of the crepe pull away from the sides of the pan. Increase the heat to medium-high and uncover the pan. Gently lift one edge of the crepe and drizzle 1 to 2 tablespoons of the oil into the pan under the crepe, taking care to avoid getting oil on the crepe itself. Lower the edge of the crepe and continue cooking, uncovered, for about 5 minutes longer, until the crepe is crispy and golden brown on the bottom.

5.
Using a rubber spatula, carefully fold the empty half of the crepe over the filling and gently transfer the folded crepe from the pan to a plate. Repeat steps 2, 3, 4, 5, and 6 with the remaining ingredients to make a total of 3 crepes, stirring the batter well before each use.

6.
Serve the crepes hot with the lettuce leaves, mint sprigs, and fish sauce on the side. To eat, cut a piece of crepe, put it on a lettuce leaf along with a few mint leaves, roll up, and dip into the fish sauce.

Bánh Bèo: Steamed Rice Cakes with Mung Beans and Shrimp

—

This classic street-food snack originated in Hue, the old imperial capital of Vietnam. This dish is all about texture: tender steamed rice cakes topped with velvety mashed mung beans that have been seasoned with a bit of pulverized, toasted dried shrimp, some fried bread cubes, and a drizzle of scallion oil. The cakes are typically steamed in small ramekins, but I've changed the recipe so it works in a muffin tin. You're going to have to jury-rig a steamer: set up a roasting pan (big enough to accommodate the muffin tin) on your stove top so it spans two burners, and use a baking sheet as a lid. In other words, improvise!

You can serve these cakes on a platter, or, if you want to get fancy, individually in oversize ceramic Asian soup spoons as hors d'oeuvres. This recipe makes about ninety bite-size cakes, which seems like a lot, but you can count on each person eating at least ten cakes—or more.

Rice Cake Batter
- 2 cups rice flour (see page 210)
- ¼ cup wheat starch
- ½ teaspoon sugar
- ¼ teaspoon salt

Toppings
- ½ cup dried mung beans (see page 207), soaked in cold water to cover overnight and drained
- 1 tablespoon fried shallots (see page 9), finely chopped
- 1½ teaspoons shallot oil (see page 9)
- 1½ teaspoons toasted and ground sesame seeds
- 1 teaspoon sugar
- ½ teaspoon kosher salt
- Pinch of ground white pepper
- ¼ cup canola oil
- ½ cup ⅛-inch-cubed white bread
- ½ cup dried shrimp (see page 205), soaked in cold water to cover overnight, drained, and pounded in a mortar with a pestle until fluffy
- Scallion oil (see page 120)
- Flavored fish sauce (see page 35), for serving

Makes about 90 bite-size cakes

1.
To make the batter, in a bowl, whisk together the rice flour, wheat starch, sugar, and salt. Add 3 cups warm water and whisk until smooth. Set aside.

2.
To prepare the toppings, bring a saucepan filled with water to a boil over high heat. Add the mung beans and cook for about 5 minutes, until very tender. Drain the beans, then spread them on paper towels in a single layer to absorb any extra liquid. Transfer to a bowl, add the fried shallots, shallot oil, sesame seeds, sugar, salt, and the white pepper. Set aside.

3.

In a small sauté pan over medium-high heat add the canola oil. When the oil is hot, add the bread cubes and fry, stirring, for about 3 to 4 minutes, until deep golden brown on all sides. Using a slotted spoon, transfer to a paper towel-lined plate and set aside. Pour off all but 1 tablespoon oil from the pan. When it is hot, add the pounded shrimp and cook, stirring constantly, for about 10 minutes, until lightly toasted. Transfer to a small bowl and set aside.

4.

Lightly spray a 12-cup standard muffin tin and a baking sheet with nonstick cooking spray

(alternatively, you can rub the interior of each muffin cup and the baking sheet with oil). Set aside. Place a roasting pan over two burners on the stove top and pour in water to a depth of ¾ inch. Turn on both burners to high.

5.

Lightly whisk the batter, then pour about 1 tablespoon of the batter into each muffin cup. When the water in the roasting pan is boiling, carefully transfer the muffin tin to the roasting pan. Cover the roasting pan tightly (a baking sheet or aluminum foil works well) and steam for about 1½ minutes, until the cakes are just set. They will begin

to pull away from the sides of the pan and take on a shiny appearance. Gently touch the top with your finger, if it's still sticky, re-cover and cook for an additional 15 to 30 seconds.

6.

Remove the muffin tin from the roasting pan and, with a spoon or small offset spatula, unmold each cake and transfer it to the prepared baking sheet. Repeat the steaming process until all of the rice batter has been used, spraying the muffin tin with nonstick cooking spray between batches and replenishing the water in the roasting pan, as needed.

8.

Shortly before you plan to serve the cakes, top each one with a scant teaspoon of the mung bean mixture and a pinch of the toasted shrimp. Top with a drizzle of scallion oil, followed by a few bread cubes. Serve immediately, accompanied with the fish sauce.

Note: To Make Ahead

The dried shrimp can be toasted in advance; they will keep in a tightly sealed container for up to 2 weeks. The mung bean mixture can be made up to 1 day ahead; refrigerate until ready to use.

Bánh Cuón: Rice Crepes with Pork and Mushrooms

—

Bánh cuón is one of the most ubiquitous street foods in Vietnam. To make it, first a rice flour batter is spread on a piece of cloth that has been stretched taut over simmering water; the resulting rice-paper circles are folded around a filling, usually pork and mushroom or sometimes a vegetarian mixture of mushrooms and water chestnuts.

When I was invited to the Masters of Food and Wine event in Carmel, California, in 1999, this was the dish I decided to make. I headed to Carmel with my cook, Mrs. Phuong, a sixty-year-old Chinese-Vietnamese woman who comes from the same town I grew up in, and a *bánh cuón* contraption that I rigged using a square of fabric, a pot, and a couple of hose clamps I picked up at Home Depot.

We probably seemed out of place—a housewife and a Vietnamese dude lugging hardware—and so they relegated us to the pastry kitchen, where Mrs. Phuong started making rice-paper wrappers by hand. It's an amazing thing to watch: as each translucent disk finishes steaming, it's peeled off the cloth with a long bamboo stick, a process that takes some experience and technique to get right. All around us, chefs from some of the country's finest restaurants were working on their foam creations, while we made one of the most humble and omnipresent of Vietnam's street foods. Before long, all of the chefs in the kitchen had stopped working and had started staring at us. They'd seen plenty of sautéing and fancy food in their careers, but they'd never seen anything like what we were doing.

Not only does this recipe require a special pot (which you can buy at some Asian kitchenware stores or make yourself; see the how-to on page 64) and a long bamboo stick (or a twelve-inch offset cake spatula), it also takes some practice to learn how thin to spread the batter on the fabric, how long to steam it, and how to peel the finished sheets from the fabric without tearing them. Other recipes recommend using a nonstick frying pan to make the rice paper, but I've never liked the results: I think you either do it the right way or you don't do it at all. This recipe works best if you have a friend helping you: one person concentrates on making the rice-paper disks and the other one fills them.

Yes, this recipe is a little challenging, but it's totally worth it. Plan to do it on a day when you have plenty of time and patience. And even if you experience disastrous results the first time you attempt the rice paper, the pork and mushroom filling is good over steamed rice.

Batter
- 3½ cups rice flour (see page 210)
- ½ cup tapioca starch (see page 212)
- 3 tablespoons potato starch
- 1½ teaspoons kosher salt

Filling
- 1 pound ground pork
- ½ cup plus 2 tablespoons canola oil
- 2 tablespoons fish sauce (see page 36)
- 1 tablespoon sugar
- 1½ teaspoons cornstarch
- 1 teaspoon freshly ground black pepper
- 1 tablespoon minced garlic
- 2 cups finely diced yellow onions
- 1½ cups finely diced fresh water chestnuts (see page 213) or jicama (see page 206)
- ¾ teaspoon kosher salt
- 1½ cups dried wood ear mushrooms, soaked in hot water to cover for about 15 minutes until softened, drained, trimmed, and finely chopped

For Serving
- 4 cups shredded red leaf lettuce
- ½ cup finely julienned spearmint
- ½ cup thinly sliced English cucumber
- ½ cup fried shallots (see page 9)
- Flavored fish sauce (see page 35)

Makes about 40 rolls, with room for error; serves 10 as an appetizer

Continued →

1.

To make the batter, in a large bowl, whisk together the rice flour, tapioca starch, potato starch, salt, and 5 cups water. Cover and refrigerate overnight. The following day, pour off all of the water from the bowl (it should measure about 2¼ cups) and replace with an equal amount of fresh water. Stir until the water is incorporated and the batter is smooth. Set aside.

2.

To make the filling, in a bowl, combine the pork, 2 tablespoons of the oil, 1 tablespoon of the fish sauce, the sugar, cornstarch, and pepper and stir to combine. Let marinate at room temperature for 15 minutes.

3.

In a large sauté pan, heat the remaining ¼ cup oil over medium heat. Add the garlic and sauté for 15 seconds. Add the onions and the pork mixture and cook, breaking up the pork with a wooden

spoon, for about 5 minutes. The pork should not brown, so lower the heat if necessary. Add the water chestnuts and salt and continue cooking for 2 minutes longer, until the pork is no longer pink and the onions are soft. Add the mushrooms and stir just to combine, then season the mixture with the remaining 1 tablespoon fish sauce. Remove from the heat and let cool completely. (The filling can be made up to 2 days in advance, cooled, covered, and refrigerated. Bring to room temperature before using.)

4.

Set up your *bánh cuốn* production line: Fill a *bánh cuốn* pot (or your makeshift pot) with water and bring to a boil over medium-high heat. Oil a rimmed baking sheet with canola oil and set aside. Oil a dinner plate and place in close proximity to the *bánh cuốn* pot. Set additional oil and a pastry brush nearby so you can oil the plate as needed. Have your pork filling at the ready.

5.

Ladle ¼ cup of the batter into the center of the fabric on the pot and, using the bottom of the ladle, quickly and gently spread the batter into a thin, even circle about 8 inches in diameter. Immediately cover the pot and let steam for 1 minute. When you uncover the pot, the rice paper should look set. Do not cook it too long or it will begin to crack.

6.

Slide a 12-inch-long offset cake spatula or bamboo stick under the edge of the rice paper farthest from you and use your thumb to anchor the center of the rice-paper sheet on the stick. Pull the stick toward you in one smooth motion, pulling the rice-paper sheet free. Transfer it to the greased plate and straighten it as needed so it is flat and wrinkle free.

7.

Spoon 2 tablespoons filling in the center of the rice-paper circle, spreading it horizontally into a rectangle about 4 inches long by 1 inch wide.

8.

Fold in the sides of the rice paper, creating right angles, then fold the bottom up and over the filling. Fold the top of the circle down so that the top edge touches the filling, then fold it a second time so the top edge of the rice paper comes up and over the filling, enclosing it completely and forming a tight little package.

9.

Transfer the roll to the prepared baking sheet. Continue making and filling the rice-paper sheets until you have used all of the batter and filling, greasing the plate as needed between batches and replenishing the water in the pot as necessary.

10.

To serve, line a platter with the shredded lettuce, mint, and cucumber and top with the rolls. Garnish with the shallots and serve the fish sauce alongside for dipping.

How to Make a Bánh Cuốn Pot

If you cannot find a *bánh cuốn* pot (which are available in some Asian markets), you can make your own from any pot that is at least 10 inches in diameter and has a domed lid. The domed lid is important because you need to cover the rice-paper sheets so they'll steam and a flat lid would smash them.

The best Western pot for the job is a pasta pot with a steamer insert. You can secure the fabric over the steamer and fill the bottom of the pot with water. If you don't have a pot like that, you can secure the fabric directly onto the pot that will contain the water, but you'll have to make a small cut into the fabric so you can add water as needed (or start with more water than you need).

- 1 pasta pot with steamer insert, 10 to 12 inches in diameter
- 1½ square feet tighly woven white fabric, preferably a 50-50 blend of cotton and polyester
- 1 (16-inch) hose clamp

1.
Lay the fabric over the top of the perforated pot insert. Attach the hose clamp, securing the fabric in place.

2.
Tighten the hose clamp with a screwdriver, pulling the fabric taut. Continue slowly until

the fabric is stretched drum-tight over the steamer insert.

3.
Trim away the excess fabric, leaving a ½-inch overhang on all sides. The pot is now ready to use. Moisten the fabric with water before each use.

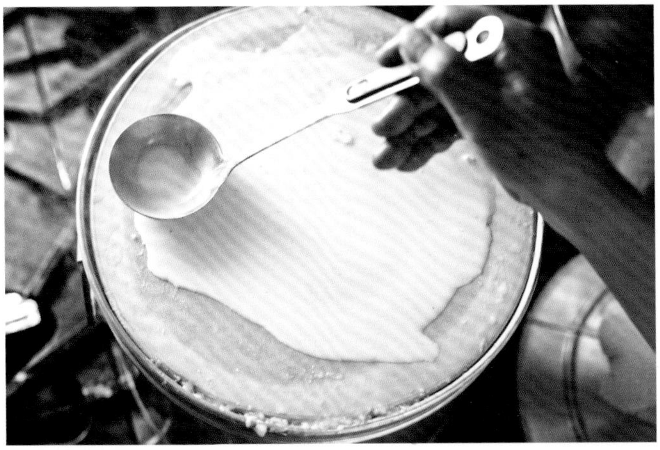
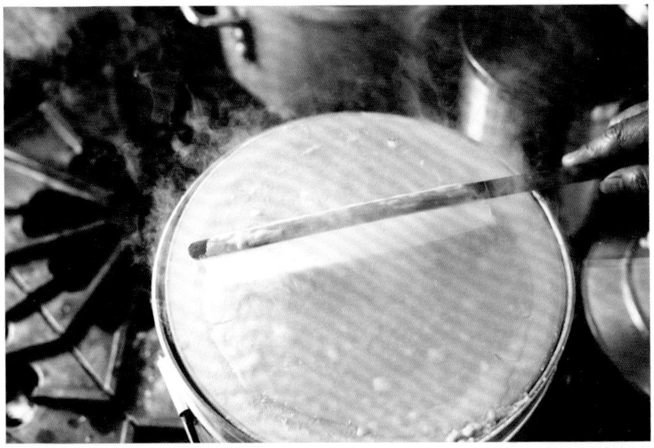
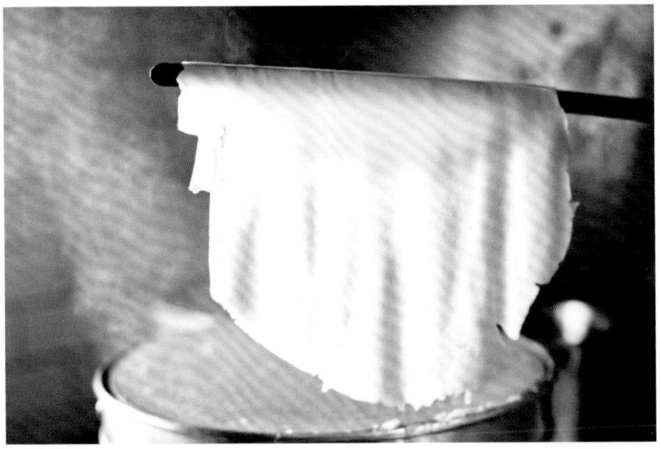
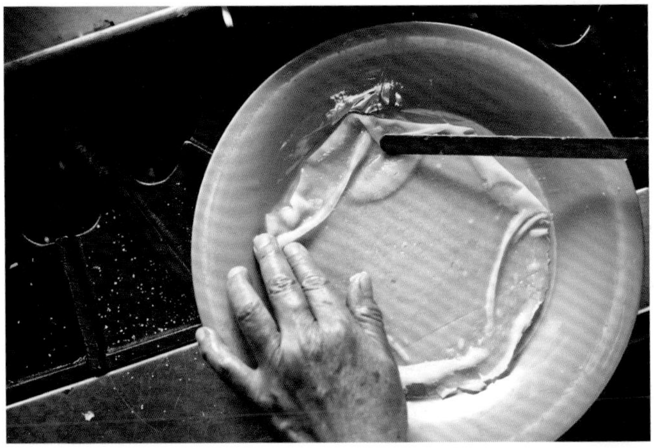
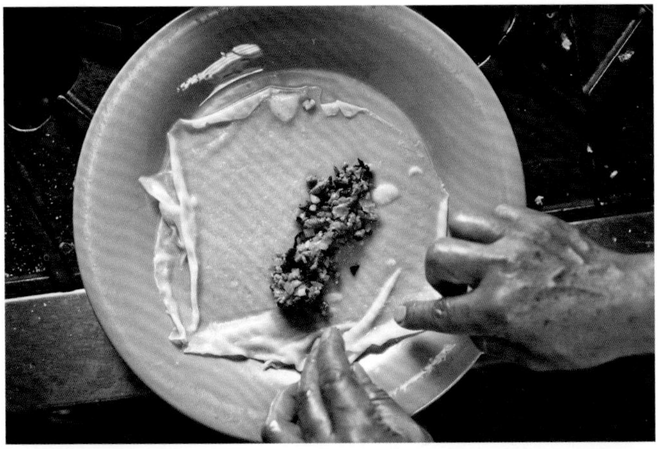
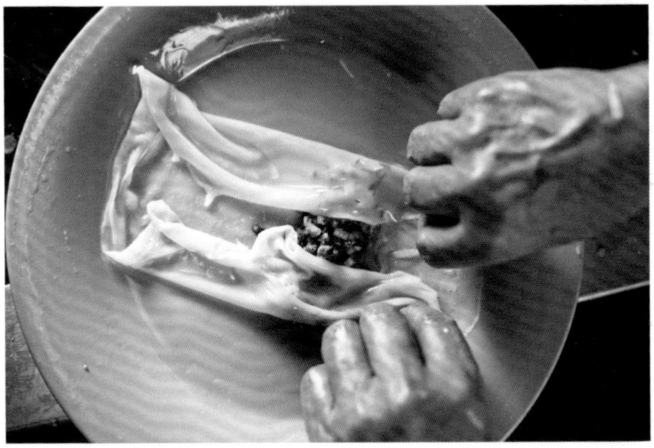
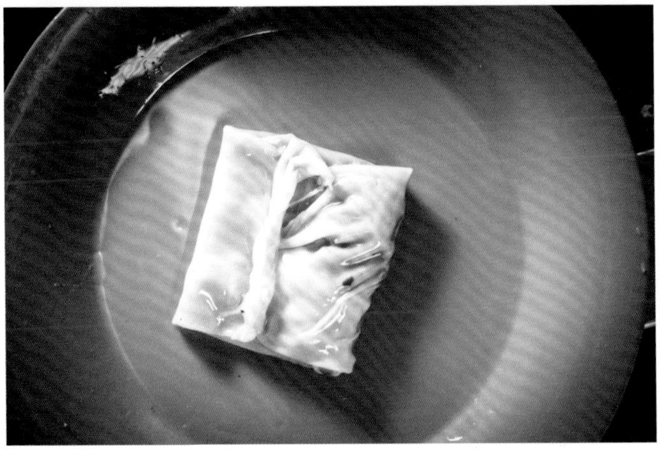
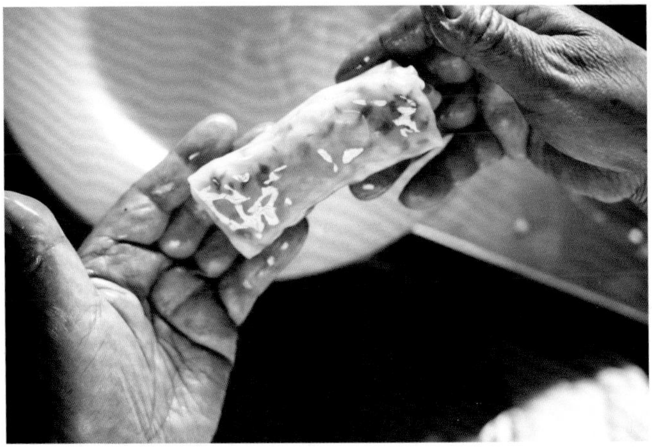

It's evening in Hanoi, and as it begins getting dark, vendors start setting up on the streets,  preparing snacks. Among them is a woman selling meat-filled buns from a makeshift steamer, the size and shape of a large metal garbage can. She works under a single bare bulb, and when she opens the lid, the air fills with a cloud of steam, evaporating into the cool night.

In the West, steaming has unfortunately gotten the reputation of being the ideal cooking technique for dieters, with vegetables the most common victims: steamed into submission and then served plain. Because of that, it is an underutilized way of preparing food in the United States.

But throughout Asia, everything is steamed, from egg custard to pork ribs to dumplings to bread. The steamer takes the place of an oven, the moist, delicate heat completely enveloping the food. Ironically, the only thing that isn't widely steamed in Vietnam is vegetables.

Steaming is one of the simplest ways of preparing food, requiring only a heat source, something to elevate the food above the water, and a tight-fitting lid. In general, it is fast, doesn't require too many dishes, and is healthful, since you don't have to add much or any oil. You can

purchase bamboo and metal steamers at any good kitchenware store, but I prefer the bamboo ones: the lids absorb moisture (so it doesn't drip back down onto your food) and they don't get too hot to handle. They're usually sold individually, and I recommend getting at least two baskets and a lid to start, so you can steam quite a number of things at once. The larger steamers (at least twelve inches in diameter) are the best, as they can accommodate everything from a whole fish to a dozen dumplings.

Bamboo steamers are ideal for dumplings and buns, fish fillets, or lotus leaf–wrapped parcels of seasoned sticky rice. They can be set over any pot of  boiling water. A wok will work, but if you steam more than you stir-fry, you'll have to be careful not to rob your wok of its nonstick patina. Any ordinary stockpot or good-size saucepan is an option. Just make sure the steamer basket fits tightly on the pot rim so no steam escapes.

For other steamed dishes, like Ground Pork with Salted Fish (page 84), the food is steamed on a rimmed dish, like a glass pie plate. You can elevate the plate above the bottom of the pot with a couple of empty tin cans with both ends removed, empty beer cans, or whatever you might have lying around the kitchen that seems like it might work. If you don't want to MacGyver it, Asian kitchenware stores also sell steaming trivets that fit inside your pot and elevate the plate above the water, or, if you are steaming in a wok, you can crisscross a pair of chopsticks inside the wok and balance the plate on the sticks. Finally, you can buy two- or three-arm plate grabbers at most kitchenware stores. While not essential, they are inexpensive and make transferring a hot plate from steamer to table much easier.

This chapter contains recipes that are prepared, start to finish, in a steamer, but Asian cooks often combine steaming with other techniques. Meat is sometimes steamed before it is fried, as in Fragrant Crispy Duck with Watercress (page 186), and for the Grilled Sweet Potatoes with Cilantro, Scallions, and Lime (page 171), the potatoes are steamed before being quickly grilled.

Steaming may be the most delicate cooking technique in the Asian repertoire, but it is also among the most versatile. There is almost nothing that can't be cooked—healthfully and quickly— with steam.

Steaming

Daikon Rice Cake with Spicy Soy
—

This is a favorite Chinese snack, found on most Cantonese dim sum menus. Vietnam, particularly in the south of the country, has a large population of people who are ethnically Chinese, like my family. My father grew up in Canton, China, but fled at age thirty-one, with his brother, during the Cultural Revolution. They ended up in Vietnam, where they started a general store in Đà Lạt. My uncle would broker for goods in Ho Chi Minh City, and my father would sell them in the store in Đà Lạt. Because many people emigrated from China just as my father and uncle did, Vietnamese food is now full of Chinese ingredients, techniques, and dishes, like this savory steamed cake.

Although many recipes for daikon rice cake contain bits of Chinese pork sausage, the version we make at The Slanted Door is vegetarian and we serve it as an appetizer. When we first added it to the menu, I honestly wasn't sure if I'd be able to sell it, but it has become one of the most frequently ordered dishes. First the cake is steamed and then panfried just before it is served. The contrast of textures—a crispy exterior and a creamy interior—adds nice dimension to the dish. It's easier to slice and fry the cake if it has cooled in the pan overnight, so plan to make this a day before you want to serve it.

- 1 cup rice flour (see page 210)
- 1 cup cornstarch
- 6 tablespoons canola oil
- 2 teaspoons minced garlic
- ⅓ cup dried shiitake mushrooms (see page 210), soaked in hot water to cover for about 15 minutes until softened, drained, stems discarded, and caps minced
- 2 tablespoons finely minced preserved turnip (see page 209)
- 2½ pounds daikon radishes (see page 204), peeled and finely grated on the small holes of a box grater
- 1 tablespoon vegetarian stir-fry sauce (optional; see page 215)
- 2 teaspoons sugar
- 1½ teaspoons kosher salt
- ¼ teaspoon freshly ground black pepper
- 1 cup spicy soy sauce (see page 71)
- Cilantro sprigs, for garnish (optional)

Makes one 9-inch round cake; serves 6 to 8 as an appetizer

1.
Oil a 9-inch round cake pan with canola oil and set aside. In a bowl, stir together the rice flour and cornstarch. Stir in 1¼ cups water, then whisk until smooth. Set aside.

2.
In a 12-inch sauté pan, heat 2 tablespoons of the oil over medium heat. Add the garlic and cook, stirring, for about 10 seconds. Add the mushrooms and preserved turnip and cook, stirring occasionally, for 3 minutes more. Transfer to a large bowl and wipe the pan clean.

3.
Return the sauté pan to medium-high heat and add 2 tablespoons of the oil. While the oil is heating, squeeze the excess water from the shredded daikon. Add the daikon, stir-fry sauce, sugar, salt, and pepper to the pan and cook, stirring occasionally, for about 10 minutes, until most of the liquid has evaporated.

4.
Remove the daikon mixture from the heat, add to the bowl with the mushroom mixture, and stir to combine. Briefly stir the rice flour-cornstarch mixture and then pour it into the bowl with the daikon and mushrooms and stir until well combined. Pour the mixture into the prepared cake pan.

5.
Pour water into a wok or stockpot and set the steamer in the wok or on the rim of the stockpot. Make sure the water does not touch the bottom of the steamer. Bring the water to a boil. When the water is boiling, place the cake pan in the steamer basket (there should be some space between the edge of the cake pan and the steamer so that steam can circulate around the pan).

Spicy Soy Sauce
—

In a bowl, stir together the sugar, soy sauce, vinegar, and ½ cup water until the sugar has dissolved. Stir in the roasted chile paste.

- ¼ cup sugar
- ½ cup light soy sauce (see page 215)
- 3 tablespoons distilled white vinegar
- 2 tablespoons roasted chile paste (see page 117)

Makes about 1½ cups

6.
Cover, and steam the cake, adding more hot water to the pot periodically as needed so it doesn't boil dry, for about 1½ hours, until lightly browned around the edges and no longer gooey in the center (press lightly with your fingertips to check; it should not stick to your fingers). Carefully remove the cake pan from the steamer and let cool for at least 2 hours at room temperature or up to overnight. If keeping overnight, let the cake cool completely at room temperature, then cover and refrigerate.

7.
When the cake has cooled, run a thin-bladed knife along the inside edge of the pan, then cut the cake into 8 wedges. With an offset spatula, remove the wedges and transfer to a plate.

8.
In a large nonstick or cast-iron frying pan, heat the remaining 2 tablespoons oil over medium heat. When the oil is shimmering but not smoking, place the cake wedges in the pan and fry, turning once, for about 10 minutes, until golden brown on both sides.

9.
Arrange the daikon cake wedges on a platter. Serve the spicy soy sauce on the side or drizzle over the fried slices. Garnish with the cilantro.

Black Bean–Glazed Pork Spareribs

—

This is a pretty classic Cantonese preparation for pork ribs, which became part of my family's repertoire thanks to my father, who came to Vietnam from Canton in 1951. Although you can buy ready-made black bean sauce at any Asian grocery store and in some supermarkets, the homemade version is free of preservatives, easy to make, and vastly superior. You'll need fermented black soybeans, which are dry-cured with salt, inexpensive, and last a long time stored in an airtight container on a cupboard shelf. They can be purchased at Asian grocery stores.

Blanching the ribs before you steam them helps to rid them of any blood or impurities, and the addition of cornstarch gives the pork a velvety texture. If you are not accustomed to steaming meat, the case with most Western cooks, you will find this technique produces especially tender, moist ribs. Serve them with steamed rice to soak up the sauce.

- 2 pounds meaty pork spareribs, cut crosswise through the bone into 1¼-inch pieces (ask your butcher to do this)
- 3 tablespoons canola oil
- 2 tablespoons fermented black beans (see page 205)
- 2 teaspoons minced garlic
- 2 tablespoons light soy sauce (see page 215)
- 2 tablespoons rice wine (see page 215)
- 2 teaspoons minced fresh ginger
- 1 teaspoon kosher salt
- 1 teaspoon cornstarch
- 1 teaspoon sugar
- 1 teaspoon freshly ground black pepper
- ½ teaspoon red pepper flakes

Serves 4 to 6 as part of a multicourse meal

1.
Prepare a large ice-water bath. Bring a large pot of water to a boil. Working in small batches, add the ribs to the boiling water and blanch for 1 minute, allowing the water to return to a boil between batches. As each batch is ready, using a slotted spoon or a spider, transfer the ribs to the ice bath to stop the cooking. When cool, scoop them out into a large bowl. Add more ice to the ice bath as needed to keep it ice-cold.

2.
In a small sauté pan, heat the oil over medium-high heat. Add the black beans and garlic and cook, stirring, for about 30 seconds, until fragrant Transfer to a small bowl, add the soy sauce, wine, ginger, salt, cornstarch, sugar, black pepper, and red pepper flakes and stir to mix well. Pour the black bean mixture over the ribs and toss well to coat evenly. Cover and let stand at room temperature for 45 minutes.

3.
Pour water into a wok or stockpot and set the steamer in the wok or on the rim of the stockpot. Make sure the water does not touch the bottom of the steamer. Bring the water to a boil.

4.
Meanwhile, place the ribs in a large rimmed plate that will fit in your steamer basket (a glass pie plate works well). When the water is boiling, place the plate in the steamer basket, cover, and steam for 25 to 30 minutes, until the ribs are cooked through.

5.
When the ribs are ready, carefully remove the plate from the steamer and serve immediately.

Bánh Nam: Banana Leaf–Wrapped Rice Dumplings

—

These flat dumplings, steamed in banana leaves, have a gentle, custardy texture and a subtly flavored filling of pork and dried shrimp. In Vietnam, they're typically sold at the markets, in part because the banana leaves make them both easy to transport and keep the dough soft and supple.

The dough is easiest to work with when it's warm, which is why I suggest you make the dumplings in two batches.

- 40 banana leaves (see page 202)
- 4 cups rice flour (see page 210)
- ¾ cup tapioca starch (see page 212)
- 2½ teaspoons kosher salt
- 1 tablespoon plus 2 teaspoons sugar
- 1 pound ground pork
- 1 tablespoon fish sauce (see page 36)
- ½ teaspoon freshly ground black pepper
- 8 tablespoons canola oil, plus more for brushing
- ½ cup dried shrimp (see page 205), soaked in cold water to cover until soft, drained
- ½ cup minced shallots
- 2 teaspoons minced garlic

Makes 20 dumplings; serves 10 as a snack or part of a multicourse meal

1.
With scissors, trim 20 of the banana leaves into 10 by 14-inch rectangles. Cut the remaining 20 banana leaves into 5 by 14-inch rectangles. Wipe each banana leaf with a damp cloth and set aside.

2.
In a large bowl, stir together the rice flour, tapioca starch, salt, 1½ teaspoons of the sugar, and 8 cups cold water. Set aside.

3.
In a bowl, combine the pork, fish sauce, pepper, and 2 tablespoons of the canola oil and mix well. Set aside.

4.
Finely chop half of the soaked, dried shrimp. In a large sauté pan, heat ¼ cup of the canola oil over medium-high heat. Add the shallots and cook, stirring, for 30 seconds. Add the garlic and cook, stirring, for 30 seconds more. Add the shrimp and cook, stirring, for 2 minutes more, until the shrimp are lightly toasted and fragrant. Add the pork mixture and 1 tablespoon sugar and cook, breaking up the pork with a wooden spoon, for about 15 minutes, until lightly browned. Remove from the heat and set aside to cool.

5.
In a heavy-bottomed 4-quart saucepan, heat 1 tablespoon of the oil over medium heat. Pour in half of the rice flour batter and cook, stirring constantly, for about 3 minutes, until it starts to thicken. Decrease the heat to low and continue whisking with a wooden spoon, until the dough has the consistency of solid vegetable shortening. Remove from the heat.

6.
Place the remaining soaked, dried shrimp in a mortar and pound with a pestle until fluffy. Transfer to a dry skillet and add the remaining ½ teaspoon salt and sugar. Cook over medium heat, stirring constantly, until shrimp are toasted and fragrant, 10 minutes.

7.
To form each dumpling, lay a large banana-leaf rectangle lengthwise on a work surface. Lay a small banana-leaf rectangle crosswise over the center of the large rectangle. Lightly brush the leaves with oil. Scoop about ⅓ cup of the warm dough onto the center of the leaves. Using your fingers, press out the dough into a rectangle about 3½ inches long, 2 inches wide, and ¼ inch thick.

8.
Spoon 1½ tablespoons of the pork mixture on top of the dough rectangle, spreading it evenly with lightly greased fingers. Sprinkle ½ teaspoon of the dried shrimp mixture evenly over pork. Fold the right and then left sides of the small banana leaf over the dough to enclose. Fold down the top of the large banana-leaf rectangle to cover the packet completely. Holding the top flap in place, bring up the bottom of the rectangle, overlapping the top flap.

9.
Fold in each side of the large banana-leaf rectangle, forming a packet.

To keep the packet from opening, turn it upside down on the work surface. Brush the exterior of the packet with a little more oil and set aside on a baking sheet. Repeat with remaining dough.

10.
When you have finished wrapping the first batch of dough in banana leaves, wash the saucepan and repeat step 5 to make a second batch of dough using the remaining oil and rice flour batter. Then, following steps 6 through 8, form packets using the second batch of dough, all of the remaining pork filling and shrimp, and the remaining banana leaves.

11.
Arrange as many of the packets as will fit in a single layer in a bamboo steamer. Pour water into a wok or stockpot, and set the steamer in the wok or on the rim of the stockpot. Make sure the water does not touch the bottom of the steamer. Cover the steamer, bring the water to a boil, and steam the packets for 12 minutes, until the dough is slightly translucent and cooked through. To test for doneness, open a packet.

12.
Remove the packets from the steamer, then steam the remaining packets the same way. Serve the packets warm.

Note: To Make Ahead
The dried shrimp can be toasted in advance; they will keep in a tightly sealed container for up to 2 weeks.

Black Cod with Lily Buds and Dried Shiitake Mushrooms

—

When The Slanted Door was relatively new and still at the original location in the Mission, this dish was one of the most frequently ordered second only to the wildly popular Shaking Beef (page 140). In those days, we made the dish with Chilean sea bass. Unfortunately the fish was so popular—and not just at our restaurant—that it has been overfished, dangerously depleting its population in most areas. When we learned that it was no longer a sustainable choice, we replaced it with black cod (also known as sablefish). This recipe requires a fatty white fish that won't dry out when cooked, yet is mild enough to absorb the subtle flavors of the sauce. Black cod fits that description and is a sustainable choice; Alaskan halibut would also work.

- 6 (5-ounce) skin-on black cod (sablefish) fillets
- ½ teaspoon freshly ground black pepper
- 6 dried shiitake mushrooms (see page 210)
- 30 dried lily buds (see page 204)
- 1 (2-ounce) package cellophane noodles (see page 12)
- 2 cups chicken stock (see page 6)
- ¼ cup light soy sauce (see page 215)
- ¼ cup plus 2 tablespoons sugar
- 3 by ½-inch piece fresh ginger, peeled and finely julienned
- 1 tablespoon shallot oil (see page 9) or canola oil
- 2 tablespoons scallion oil (optional; see page 120), for garnish
- ¼ cup julienned scallions, for garnish
- 12 small cilantro sprigs, for garnish

Serves 6 as a main course

1.
Season the fish fillets lightly with the pepper and set aside. Put the shiitake mushrooms and lily buds in separate bowls, add hot water to cover to both bowls, and let soak for about 15 minutes, until softened. Drain the lily buds, trim away the tough end from each bud, and set aside. Drain the mushrooms, remove and discard the stems, thinly slice the caps, and set aside.

2.
Place the cellophane noodles in a bowl, add very hot water to cover, and let stand for 10 to 15 minutes, until softened. Drain and set aside.

3.
In a bowl, whisk together the stock, soy sauce, sugar, and 1 cup water until the sugar has dissolved. Set aside.

4.
Pour water into a wok or stockpot and set one tier of a two-tiered steamer in the wok or on the rim of the stockpot. Make sure the water does not touch the bottom of the steamer. Remove the steamer and bring the water to a boil over high heat.

5.
Meanwhile, divide the shiitake mushrooms, lily buds, and cellophane noodles evenly between 2 rimmed dishes that will fit inside your steamer (glass pie plates work well). Top each with half of the ginger and 3 pieces of fish. Divide the stock-soy mixture evenly between the dishes, and drizzle the shallot oil over the fish, again dividing it evenly.

6.
Place a dish in each bamboo tier and place over the boiling water. Cover and steam for 6 to 8 minutes, until the fish flakes easily when touched with the tip of a knife.

7.
Uncover the top steamer and carefully transfer the dishes holding the fish, to two large round platters. Garnish each piece of fish with a spoonful of scallion oil, some scallion, and 2 cilantro sprigs. Serve immediately.

Chicken Steamed Buns

—

These buns are a direct import from China, one the Vietnamese have happily embraced. They are usually filled with a bit of meat and typically served for breakfast alongside a cup of tea or warm soy milk.

Instead of using a starter, which is how the dough is typically made in Southern China, this recipe calls for yeast, which is the style in Northern China, and also easier for the home cook. The end result is not as fluffy, but the dough is much easier to shape. Working with the dough takes a little practice. The goal is to roll out rounds that are thinner on the edges and thicker in the center, so that when you pinch the dough around the filling you can form a sort of small topknot. It may take a few batches to get the hang of forming the buns, but you can always eat the less-than-perfect early attempts.

Dough
- 4 tablespoons sugar
- 1 cup warm water
- 1¼ teaspoons instant yeast
- 3¼ cups all purpose flour
- 2 tablespoons canola oil, plus more for oiling bowl
- 1¼ teaspoons baking powder

Filling
- ½ pound skinless, boneless chicken thighs, finely diced
- ¼ cup finely diced yellow onion
- ¼ cup finely diced stemmed fresh shiitake mushrooms (about 3 mushrooms)
- ¼ cup fried shallots (see page 9)
- 3 tablespoons canola oil
- 2 tablespoons chopped fresh cilantro
- 1 tablespoon minced scallion, light green part only
- 1¼ teaspoons finely minced fresh ginger
- 1¼ teaspoons fish sauce (see page 36)
- 1 teaspoon toasted, ground sesame seeds
- ½ teaspoon kosher salt
- 1 teaspoon oyster sauce (see page 214)
- 1 teaspoon toasted sesame oil
- ¼ teaspoon freshly ground black pepper
- 1 egg white

- 10 3 by 3-inch squares of parchment paper

Makes 10 buns; serves 10 as a snack or part of a multicourse meal

1.
In a small bowl, combine the sugar and water and stir until the sugar dissolves. Sprinkle the yeast over and let stand 10 minutes until foamy.

2.
Sift the flour into a bowl and stir in the water mixture. Stir with a wooden spoon just until the dough comes together into a shaggy, sticky ball, then turn the dough out onto a well-floured surface, drizzle the dough with the oil, and knead until the dough is smooth and has the texture of an earlobe, about 10 minutes (this can also be done in an electric mixer fitted with the dough hook attachment).

3.
Lightly oil a large bowl and place the dough in the bowl, turning to coat on all sides with oil. Cover with a clean, dry kitchen towel and let stand in a warm place until doubled in size, about 2 hours.

4.
While the dough rises, make the filling. In a large bowl, combine all ingredients and mix well.

5.
Punch down the dough and turn out onto a floured surface. Sprinkle the baking powder over the surface of the dough, then gently knead until well incorporated. Divide the dough into 10 even balls (each about 2½ ounces) and cover with a clean, dry kitchen towel.

6.
Working with one ball of dough at a time, with a rolling pin, start from the center of the disk outward, roll out the dough into a round 3½ inches in diameter that is slightly thicker in the center than it is around the edges. As you work, lift and rotate the dough occasionally to prevent sticking.

Continued →

7.
Place the dough round on your nondominant hand, cupping your hand slightly. Using your dominant hand, spoon about 3 tablespoons of the chicken filling into the center of the round. Take care not to get any filling on the edge of the round, which would make sealing the bun difficult. Pull the edges of the dough up and around the filling to enclose it, pleating and twisting slightly to seal and form a small topknot. Transfer to a lightly oiled baking sheet and cover with a clean dish towel. Fill the remaining dough balls the same way. Let the finished buns stand for 30 minutes before steaming. Just before steaming, place each bun on a square of parchment paper.

8.
Pour water into a wok or stockpot and set one tier of a two-tiered steamer in the wok or on the rim of the stockpot. Make sure the water does not touch the bottom of the steamer. Remove the steamer and bring the water to a boil over high heat.

9.
Meanwhile, arrange the buns in two bamboo tiers, spacing them about 1 inch apart, then place over the boiling water. Cover and steam for 15 to 20 minutes, until the dough is puffed and has a slightly shiny appearance and the filling has cooked through. To check for doneness, insert a metal skewer or the tip of a thin-bladed knife into the center of a bun and then touch the metal to your fingertip; it should be very hot.

10.
Transfer each tier of the steamer to a plate and serve the buns directly from the steamer.

Note: To Freeze
The buns can be frozen for up to a month. Freeze them on a baking sheet in a single layer. When completely frozen, transfer to a resealable plastic bag and store in the freezer. You do not need to thaw before steaming; just increase the steaming time by 5 minutes.

Vegetarian Steamed Buns

—

We make a vegetarian filling that is heavy on the mushrooms, with cellophane noodles and cabbage to add body and texture. We like to use white beech mushrooms, but if you cannot find them, you could substitute, king trumpet or oyster mushrooms, or any other firm, meaty variety.

- Dough for Chicken Steamed Buns (see page 78)
- 2 ounces dried cellophane noodles (see page 12)
- 2 tablespoons canola oil
- 1 cup fresh wood ear mushrooms, julienned
- 1½ cups *hon shimeji* (white beech) or oyster mushrooms, cut into small pieces
- 1 cup thinly sliced green cabbage
- ⅓ cup finely diced fresh water chestnuts (see page 213) or jicama (see page 206)
- 1½ tablespoons vegetarian stir-fry sauce (see page 215)
- ¼ teaspoon toasted sesame oil
- ¼ teaspoon sugar
- ¼ teaspoon kosher salt
- ⅛ teaspoon freshly ground black pepper

Makes 10 buns; serves 10 as a snack or part of a multicourse meal

1.
Make the dough and set aside to rise as directed.

2.
Place the cellophane noodles in a bowl, add very hot water to cover, and let stand for 10 to 15 minutes, until softened. Drain and set aside.

3.
In a large frying pan, heat the oil over high heat. When the oil is shimmering but not smoking, add all of the mushrooms and sauté for 4 to 5 minutes, until slightly softened. Add the cabbage and sauté for 3 to 5 minutes longer, until the cabbage has just wilted.

4.
Remove from the heat and transfer to a large bowl. Add the water chestnuts, noodles, stir-fry sauce, sesame oil, sugar, salt, and pepper and stir to mix well. Taste and adjust the seasoning if needed. Spread the filling out on a rimmed baking sheet and let cool completely.

5.
Fill, steam, and serve the buns as directed for the chicken-filled buns (see page 78).

Pork Steamed Buns

—

The pork buns that you usually find are filled with garish red cubes of sweet barbecued pork that have been colored with food coloring. We skip the dye and dial back the sugar, instead seasoning the pork with soy and oyster sauces, chile, sesame oil and preserved turnip. The pork has to marinate overnight, so plan accordingly. The filling can also be made in advance, transferred to a plastic storage bag and frozen for up to three months; defrost it before using.

- Dough for Chicken Steamed Buns (see page 78)
- ⅔ cup plus 1 teaspoon of sugar
- ¼ cups plus 1 teaspoon fish sauce (see page 36)
- 1 tablespoon plus 1 teaspoon minced garlic
- 1 tablespoon minced shallots
- 1 Thai chile, stemmed and finely chopped
- ¼ teaspoon freshly ground black pepper
- 1 pound boneless pork shoulder
- ⅓ cup preserved turnip (see page 209)
- 1½ tablespoons canola oil
- 2 teaspoons toasted sesame oil
- 1 by ½-inch piece fresh ginger, peeled and finely chopped
- ⅔ cup yellow onion, thinly sliced
- 4 scallions, white part only, julienned
- ¼ cup fried shallots (see page 9)
- 1 tablespoon oyster sauce (see page 214)
- 1 tablespoon light soy sauce (see page 215)
- 2 tablespoons dark soy sauce (see page 215)

Makes 10 buns; serves 10 as a snack or part of a multicourse meal

1.
Make the dough and set aside to rise as directed.

2.
To make the filling, in a bowl, combine ¼ cup fish sauce, ⅔ cup sugar, garlic, shallot, chile, and the pepper and whisk until the sugar has dissolved. Put the pork in a resealable plastic bag and pour the fish sauce mixture into the bag. Seal the bag and refrigerate overnight.

3.
The next day, preheat the oven to 375°F. Line a rimmed baking sheet with aluminum foil. Lift the pork out of the marinade and discard the marinade. Arrange the pork on the prepared pan.

4.
Roast for 25 to 30 minutes, until an instant-read thermometer inserted into the thickest part of the pork registers 140°F. Remove from the oven, let cool to room temperature, then dice finely. Transfer to a large bowl and set aside.

5.
In a small saucepan, combine the preserved turnip with water to cover and bring to a boil over high heat. Boil for 20 minutes, then drain and rinse well with cold water. Finely dice the turnip.

6.
In a sauté pan, heat half of the canola oil over medium heat. Add the remaining 1 teaspoon garlic and cook for 10 seconds. Add the turnip, the remaining 1 teaspoon fish sauce, 1 teaspoon of the sesame oil, and the remaining teaspoon of sugar and cook for 1 minute more. Transfer to the bowl with the pork and wipe the pan clean.

7.
Return the sauté pan to the stove top, add the remaining oil, and heat over medium heat. Add the ginger and yellow onion and cook, stirring occasionally, for about 6 minutes, until soft. Stir in the scallions and cook, stirring, for 3 minutes more.

8.
Remove from the heat and pour off any excess oil from the pan. Add the fried shallots, 2 tablespoons water, the remaining teaspoon sesame oil, the oyster sauce, and the light and dark soy sauces and stir to mix well. Transfer the mixture to a blender or food processor and process until smooth. Taste and adjust the seasoning with salt if needed. Add to the bowl containing the pork and turnips and mix well.

9.
Fill, steam, and serve the buns as directed for the chicken-filled buns (see page 78).

Ground Pork with Salted Fish
—

This dish, which has roots in China, is one that my mother used to make for me when I was a kid. Now it's a favorite of my own kids and we probably eat it once a week. The seasoned ground pork has the appeal of sausage, and the addition of cornstarch helps to both bind the hand-chopped pork and give it a silky texture. The fish adds salty, savory flavor, but it's not overwhelmingly fishy. Whole salted mackerel are available in Asian grocery stores, but if you can't find them, you can substitute jarred anchovy fillets. This dish is simple and quick to make. Invite diners to spoon portions of it over a bowl of steamed rice.

- 12 ounces boneless pork shoulder, hand-chopped (see page 52), or coarsely ground pork
- 2 teaspoons finely chopped garlic
- ¼ cup finely diced fresh water chestnuts (see page 213) or jicama (see page 206)
- 3 fresh shiitake mushrooms, stemmed and finely chopped
- 1 tablespoon fish sauce (see page 36)
- 3 teaspoons canola oil
- 1 teaspoon cornstarch
- Pinch of kosher salt
- Pinch of freshly ground black pepper
- 2 by 1 by ½-inch piece dried salted mackerel, or 3 jarred anchovy fillets
- 2 by ½-inch piece fresh ginger, peeled and finely julienned

Serves 4 to 6 as part of a multicourse meal

1.
Pour water into a wok or stockpot and set the steamer in the wok or on the rim of the stockpot. Make sure the water does not touch the bottom of the steamer. Cover the steamer and bring the water to a boil over high heat.

2.
Meanwhile, in a bowl, combine the pork, garlic, water chestnuts, mushrooms, fish sauce, 1 teaspoon of the oil, the cornstarch, salt, and pepper. Stir just until evenly mixed.

3.
Oil a rimmed heatproof plate (a glass pie plate works well) with ½ teaspoon of the oil. Press the pork onto the plate, forming a large, thin patty. Place the mackerel in the center of the patty; sprinkle the ginger evenly over the top and drizzle evenly with the remaining 1½ teaspoons oil.

4.
Place the dish in the steamer, re-cover, and steam for 15 to 20 minutes, until the meat is no longer pink. Carefully remove the plate from the steamer and serve immediately.

Hue Rice Dumplings
—

I like to call these dumplings Vietnamese Gummi bears. The wrapper is made from tapioca starch and rice flour, which give it a springy, chewy texture that contrasts well with the rich, savory mung bean filling. Although the name indicates that these dumplings originated in the former imperial capital of Hue, I first had them in Hoi An, once an important port but now a popular tourist spot.

When I'm traveling and I taste something really delicious in the market, it's not uncommon for me to go back to eat it a second or third time. After I tried these chewy dumplings the first time in Hoi An, I returned to the market the next day to eat them again. On both of those occasions, the dumplings were filled with a mixture of shrimp and pork. On the third day, the town was celebrating a Buddhist holiday, and every single vendor, except for the roast duck lady, was offering only vegetarian food. The dumpling vendor had replaced the meat filling with one made from mashed mung beans seasoned with shallot oil and not much else. I ended up liking that version even more, so I owe this recipe to the Buddhists. In addition to being vegetarian, this dish is also vegan.

Filling
- 6 tablespoons dried mung beans (see page 207), soaked in cold water to cover overnight
- ¼ cup sesame seeds, toasted
- ½ cup fried shallots (see page 9), minced
- ¼ cup shallot oil (see page 9)
- ½ teaspoon kosher salt
- 2 teaspoons sugar

Dough
- 2⅓ cups tapioca starch (see page 212), plus more for dusting
- ½ cup cornstarch
- ½ cup rice flour (see page 210)
- 1 tablespoon sugar
- 1½ teaspoons kosher salt
- ¼ cup plus 2 tablespoons shallot oil (see page 9)

Flavored Soy Sauce
- ½ cup light soy sauce (see page 215)
- 1½ tablespoons distilled white vinegar
- ¼ cup plus 1 tablespoon sugar
- 1 small clove garlic, minced
- 1 to 2 Thai chiles, stemmed and minced

- Scallion oil (see page 120), for drizzling

Makes about 80 bite-size dumplings; serves 6 to 10 as a snack or appetizer

1.
Pour water into a wok or stockpot and set a two-tiered bamboo steamer in the wok or on the rim of the stockpot. Make sure the water does not touch the bottom of the steamer. Line the steamer with a round of parchment. Cover and bring to a boil over high. Drain the mung beans and spread in parchment-lined steamer. Cover and steam until pale yellow and soft, about 20 minutes. Remove from the heat, transfer to a rimmed baking sheet and refrigerate until cool.

2.
Put the sesame seeds in a food processor and pulse until ground. Add the cooled mung beans, fried shallots, shallot oil, salt, and sugar and pulse until well blended. Set the filling aside.

3.
To make the dough, in a small saucepan or a kettle, bring 2 cups water to a boil. Meanwhile, in a bowl, whisk together the tapioca starch, cornstarch, rice flour, sugar, and salt. When the water is boiling, gradually add it to the flour mixture while stirring constantly. Then add the shallot oil and knead it into the flour mixture with your hands until a smooth dough forms. The texture will be sticky and gooey, like taffy or melted mozzarella.

4.
Dust a work surface with 1 tablespoon tapioca starch. Transfer the dough to the floured surface and knead for about 5 minutes, until it is smooth and soft, dusting the surface with additional tapioca starch as necessary to prevent the dough from sticking. It will have the texture and appearance of modeling clay. Divide the dough into 6 equal portions and cover them with plastic wrap.

Continued →

5.
Remove 1 portion of the dough from under the plastic wrap, leaving the others covered. Dust your work surface with tapioca starch and, using your palms, roll the dough back and forth on the work surface into a log 13 inches long and 1 inch in diameter. Cut the log crosswise into 13 even pieces. Cover the pieces with plastic wrap. Repeat with the remaining dough portions, making sure to cover all of the pieces as they are cut.

6.
Lightly oil 2 rimmed baking sheets. To fill the dumplings, lightly flour your fingers with tapioca starch and, working with one piece of dough at a time (keeping the rest covered) roll the dough into a ball. Gently press the ball into a round about 2 inches wide. Place ½ teaspoon of the filling in the center of the dough round, fold the round in half, and pinch the edges together to seal. Repeat with the remaining dough pieces and filling. As the dumplings are formed, place them on the prepared baking sheets and cover with plastic wrap.

7.
Meanwhile, arrange as many dumplings as will fit in a single layer in each parchment-lined bamboo tier, spacing them so they don't touch. Return the water to a boil, then cover and steam. Cover and steam the dumplings for 6 to 8 minutes, until translucent and slightly shiny.

8.
While the dumplings are steaming, make the dipping sauce. In a small bowl, stir together the soy sauce, ¼ cup water, the vinegar, and sugar until the sugar has dissolved. Stir in the garlic and chiles.

9.
When the dumplings are ready, remove the bamboo tiers from over the water and, using chopsticks or your fingers, carefully transfer them to a warmed large platter. Drizzle the dumplings with shallot oil and serve the flavored soy sauce alongside. Repeat the steaming process with the remaining dumplings, replacing the parchment rounds for each new batch.

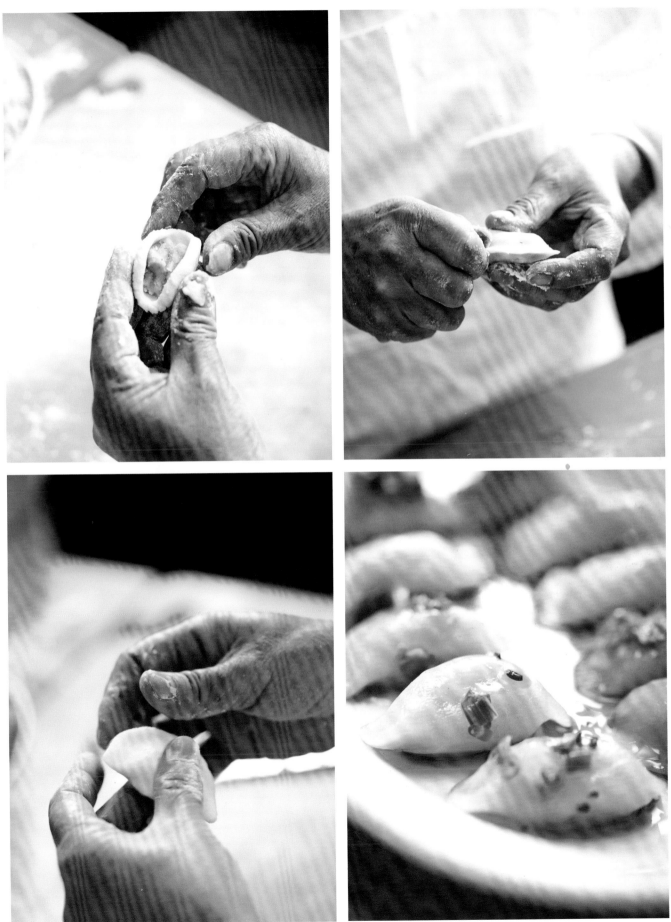

Lotus Leaf–Wrapped Sticky Rice

—

This dish typically shows up in Vietnam in September, during the harvest festivals. When I was a kid, I was told a story about a high-ranking officer who had done a good deed and then soon after died tragically in a drowning accident. The dragon boat races held during the harvest festival were a way of honoring his memory. People would throw these rice parcels into the river in a show of respect for his heroism and so he'd have something to eat in the afterlife.

To make the parcels, sticky rice, flavored with bits of mushroom, fried taro, and tofu is tightly wrapped in lotus leaves, forming something that resembles a Mexican tamale. The neatly wrapped packages are portable and filling, good for lunch boxes and camping trips, and when you open one, the rice is permeated with the fragrance of the lotus leaves.

This recipe calls for Golden Mountain seasoning sauce, a soybean-based product made in Thailand that is similar to soy sauce but a bit saltier (and sweeter, as it contains some sugar). It is used with abandon in Thailand and can be purchased here in Asian grocery stores.

- 5 cups sweet (glutinous) rice (see page 211)
- 2 teaspoons kosher salt
- 4 teaspooons sugar
- 1 cup dried shiitake mushrooms (see page 210)
- ¼ cup canola oil, plus more for deep-frying
- 1 cup peeled and diced taro (see page 212)
- 1 cup diced medium-firm tofu
- 1 cup diced fresh water chestnuts (see page 213) or jicama (see page 206)
- 1 cup diced oyster mushrooms
- 1½ tablespoons porcini powder (optional; see page 209)
- ½ teaspoon freshly ground black pepper
- ½ cup plus 1 tablespoon vegetarian stir-fry sauce (see page 215)
- 3 tablespoons Golden Mountain seasoning sauce (see page 214)
- 1 cup diced yellow onion
- 2 teaspoons toasted sesame oil
- 12 dried lotus leaves, soaked in warm water to cover for about 10 minutes until soft and pliable, drained, and patted dry

Makes 12 wrapped rice dumplings; serves 6 as a snack, appetizer, or light lunch

1.
To make the filling, put the rice in a fine-mesh sieve and rinse well under cold running water. Transfer the rice to a large saucepan, add 5 cups water, and let soak for 2 hours.

2.
Add 1 teaspoon of salt and 2 teaspoons of the sugar to the rice and its soaking water, place the pan over medium heat, and bring to a boil. Stir to mix, lower the heat so the liquid is at a gentle simmer, cover, and simmer for about 20 minutes, until the water is absorbed and the rice is tender. Uncover, fluff the rice with a fork, and then spread on a rimmed baking sheet to cool.

3.
In a bowl, soak the shiitake mushrooms in hot water to cover for about 15 minutes, until softened. Drain, remove and discard the stems, and thinly slice the caps. Set aside.

4.
In a heavy-bottomed saucepan, pour the canola oil to a depth of 2 inches and heat over medium-high heat to 350°F on a deep-frying thermometer. Add the taro and fry, stirring occasionally, for about 10 minutes, or until golden brown. Using a slotted spoon, transfer to paper towels to drain.

5.
Return the oil to 350°F, add the tofu, and fry for about 10 minutes, until golden brown. Using the slotted spoon, transfer to paper towels to drain.

6.
In a large bowl, combine the taro, tofu, water chestnuts, oyster mushrooms, porcini powder, pepper, and the remaining 2 teaspoons sugar and 1 teaspoon salt. Mix well and set aside.

7.
In a small bowl, stir together the stir-fry and seasoning sauces.

8.
In a large sauté pan, heat ¼ cup oil over medium-high heat. Add the onion and cook, stirring occasionally, for about 3 minutes, until soft. Add the shiitakes and sauté for 1 minute more. Add the taro mixture and the sauce mixture, stir to combine, and cook for 2 minutes longer. Stir in the sesame oil and transfer to a large bowl. Set aside.

9.
In a blender, combine ½ cup water and ½ cup of the taro mixture and process until smooth. Pour this mixture into the bowl containing the remaining taro mixture and stir to mix well.

10.
Place a lotus leaf on your work surface with the tapered edge closest to you. Measure ⅓ cup of the cooked rice and pat it between your hands into a patty about 3 inches in diameter and ¼ inch thick (like making a hamburger patty). Make a second rice patty in the same fashion. Holding a patty in your nondominant hand,

spoon ¼ cup of the taro filling onto the center of it. Top with the second rice patty, enclosing the filling, and then squeeze the patties with your hand to form them into a ball. Repeat with remaining rice and filling, transferring finished balls to a lightly greased baking sheet.

11.
Place the rice ball in the center of the lotus leaf and flatten slightly with your hands. Pull the right side of the leaf up and over to cover the ball, and then do the same with left side of the leaf. Bring the

tapered edge of the lotus leaf up and over the ball and then continue to wrap until you have formed a tight parcel. Repeat with remaining rice balls.

12.
Pour water into a wok or stockpot and bring to a boil over high heat.

13.
Divide the lotus parcels between two bamboo steamer tiers, then place over the boiling water. Cover and steam for about 12 minutes, until heated through. Transfer to a platter and let diners unwrap.

Steamed Whole Fish with Ginger, Scallions, and Soy

—

This is a simple way to prepare whole fish, yet one that few Western cooks have mastered. In the Vietnamese culture, a properly steamed fish is a benchmark for chefs, and those who can't do it right are considered to be bad cooks. A perfectly steamed fish has flesh that is just cooked at the bone, never dry. Typically, whole fish are not served with the liquid in which it was steamed, which is too fishy tasting, and any sauce is added at the end, after the fish has been cooked. In this classic Chinese preparation, the fish is topped with scallions, cilantro and ginger, then doused with hot oil, which releases the flavor of the aromatics into the flesh of the fish.

- 1 (1½-pound) whole white fish (such as sea bass, branzino, or flounder), cleaned with head and tail intact
- Kosher salt and freshly ground black pepper
- 2 by ½-inch piece fresh ginger, peeled and finely julienned
- ¼ cup light soy sauce (see page 215)
- 1 tablespoon rice wine (see page 215)
- 1 scallion, white and light green parts only, julienned
- 4 cilantro sprigs
- ½ cup canola oil

Serves 2 to 4 as part of a multicourse meal

1.
Rinse the fish in cold water and pat dry with paper towels. Season the fish inside and out with salt and pepper. Place the fish on a heatproof plate that is both large enough to accommodate it (a glass pie plate works well) and will also fit inside your steamer, bending the fish slightly if it is too long. Stuff half of the ginger inside the cavity of the fish and spread the remaining ginger on top of the fish.

2.
Pour water into a wok or stockpot and set a steamer in the wok or on the rim of the stockpot. Make sure the water does not touch the bottom of the steamer. Bring the water to a boil over high heat.

3.
Place the plate holding the fish in the steamer, cover, and steam for about 8 minutes, until the fish flakes easily when tested with the tip of a knife.

4.
While the fish is steaming, in a small bowl, stir together the soy sauce, wine, and 1 tablespoon of water. Set aside.

5.
When the fish is ready, carefully remove the plate from the steamer and pour off any accumulated liquid. Lay the scallion and cilantro along the top of the fish. In a small sauté pan, heat the oil over high heat until it is hot but not smoking. Remove the oil from the heat and pour it directly over the scallion and cilantro to "cook" them. Drizzle the soy mixture over the fish and serve immediately.

How to Prepare a Whole Fish

Most markets sell fish that have already been scaled and gutted. If a fish has not been cleaned, you can the fishmonger to clean it for you. When we serve a whole fish at the restaurants, we also trim off the fins because the fish is easier to serve without them. With a pair of scissors, cut off the fins from both sides of the fish, from the belly, and then the dorsal fins (the ones running along the back). Finally, trim the tail by cutting it into a V shape and score the fish.

Braising

Most of us know braising as a way to cook meat in stock for a long period of time. In Vietnam, there are two types of braised dishes: the classic braise, where the meat or fish is nearly submerged in liquid, and what is called a dry braise, *ko* in Vietnamese, where the ingredients are cooked in a smaller amount of liquid, often caramel sauce. In this chapter, we include recipes for both styles of braises.

Most—but not all—braises begin with browning the meat. Then aromatics and liquid—stock, wine, beer, coconut milk, or

even water—are added and the pot is left to cook over gentle heat until the connective tissue and fat in the meat break down, giving it a silky texture and the liquid a rich, robust, deep flavor. In a Vietnamese braise, the same basic principles apply, but in addition to the aromatics commonly found in a Western braise, such as onions and garlic, Vietnamese cooks often include lemongrass, chiles, and ginger. They also use fish sauce in place of table salt for seasoning, and often water is the liquid of choice, which results in a lighter, brothier finished product, rather than meat in a thick sauce. And unlike many Western braises that begin on the stove top and are finished in a low oven, Vietnamese braises are cooked entirely on the stove top. That's because, as already noted, most Vietnamese kitchens don't have ovens.

Braising may not be the first technique you think of when you think of Asian cooking, but braised dishes are common, even in tropical places, as one element of a multicourse meal. Offset by fresher salads and stir-fried greens, the braised meat or fish is used almost as a condiment for the other dishes, with the richly flavored sauce spooned over rice.

In most of Asia, and in many other parts of the world, the pots traditionally used for braising are made from clay. Yes, you have to season a clay pot before you can use it (read all about how to select and season a clay pot on page 99), and yes, a clay pot is more delicate than a cast-iron pan and will probably break one day and have to be replaced. That's why they are usually not too expensive.

In spite of these inconveniences, a clay pot is the ideal vessel for braising for three

good reasons: the thick clay walls help maintain even heat throughout the cooking time, the vessel itself is beautiful, and the pot can go straight from the stove to the table, where it will keep food warmer longer. If you use a clay pot, however, you will have to brown the meat in a separate pan. It is impossible to get a clay pot hot enough to do the job without it breaking. If I have failed to convince you to add some clay pots to your collection, all of these recipes can be made in a Dutch oven or any heavy-bottomed pot (the heavy bottom is important to prevent scorching). If you have browned the ingredients in a metal pot, you can just continue cooking the recipe in that pot.

For the most part, braising is slow cooking, and the cook's time is mostly lazy and inactive. The pot is left to simmer on the stove, filling your house with the good smells of Lemongrass Beef Stew (page 115) or Soy-Braised Pork Belly (page 106). But there are a few quicker braises, too, like Caramelized Lemongrass Shrimp (page 116) and Chicken with Lily Buds and Dried Shiitake Mushrooms (page 100), both of which can be made in under an hour, start to finish.

How to Choose and Use a Cleaver
—

Cleavers are ubiquitous in Asian kitchens, but not all cleavers are alike. There are heavy, thick cleavers that are used to hack through meat and bone, and smaller, snub-nosed versions with thin blades for slicing vegetables.

When you are selecting a cleaver, consider its intended use. If its primary purpose will be cutting up chickens and chopping through pork ribs, buy one with a thick blade that has some weight to it. The lighter, thinner cleavers would be completely destroyed by those tasks. A heavy cleaver is also handy for crushing ginger, garlic cloves, and lemongrass stalks. Some meat cleavers cost upward of one hundred dollars, which is an enormous waste of money. No matter how well you care for your knives, a meat cleaver will take a beating. A heavy-duty version that you find at a restaurant-supply store (not a fancy kitchenware store) is perfect and will cost you about $20.

If you'll be mostly using your cleaver to slice vegetables and julienne ginger, you'll want to purchase one of the smaller, lighter types, which are much easier to manipulate and won't tire your wrist out. These knives are real kitchen workhorses: you can slice with them, use a flat side to crush ginger and garlic and transfer chopped food to a pan, and use the blunt back edge to tenderize meat.

My preference is for carbon steel which sharpens more easily than stainless steel and holds a fine edge. They do need care, however, as they rust easily and must be sharpened more often.

To use a cleaver, grab it by the handle with your dominant hand. Choke up on the blade by moving your hand to the top of the handle close to the blade, then put your thumb on one side of the blade and your index finger on the opposite side. With your other three fingers, grip the cleaver handle. This will give you the most control over the knife and keep your arm from getting tired.

Clay Pots
—

I was a budding ceramicist when I was younger. The summer after eighth grade, I helped my art teacher move into a new classroom, and in exchange he showed me how to use the potter's wheel. I was hooked, and spent the next four years of high school making ceramics, even winning some awards in high school. I considered going to art school to further my study, but my father stepped in and "redirected" me into the architecture program at UC Berkeley. When we opened The Slanted Door, I went to Chiang Mai, Thailand, to select pottery to use at the restaurant. We still serve our food on ceramics today.

In my home kitchen, I have a pretty sizable collection of clay pots of all shapes and sizes: wire-encased Chinese-style sand pots, elegant hollow-handled Japanese pots, rough-hewn Egyptian pots, a hand-painted conical Moroccan *tagine*. There's one compelling reason to start a collection of your own: clay pots are beautiful.

But they offer more than good looks. They are highly functional, particularly for slow-cooked dishes. The transfer of heat is completely different from what you get with steel or any other metal. In clay, it is slow, even, and gentle. When you braise in a clay pot, you also lose more liquid, which results in a sauce that is more concentrated in both flavor and texture. Some people say that the clay imparts a flavor to the finished dish, but I've never noticed this to be true.

As I noted earlier, clay pots aren't as sturdy as heavy Dutch ovens (which are fine substitutes), though following a few simple rules will extend their lives. First, always use a heat diffuser on the stove top to ensure gentle, even heat. It's also a good idea to start the pot off over low heat and then gradually increase it to the desired level. And never add cold liquid to a hot clay pot, which will cause it to expand and shatter. But even with these precautions, it's best to use a clay pot over no higher than medium heat, another reason why these beautiful pots are well suited to braising.

Braising

How to Season a New Clay Pot

You need to season any clay pot before you use it for the first time on the stove top, a simple step that will help prevent cracking and make the pot generally more durable. First, immerse the pot in cold water to cover and let soak for 2 hours. Remove the pot from the water, dry it well, and coat any unglazed surface (usually the bottom exterior of the pot) with canola or other neutral-tasting oil. Fill the pot three-fourths full with water. Now you can finish the seasoning on the stove top or in the oven. To finish on the stove top, put a heat diffuser on a burner, place the water-filled pot on top, turn the heat on to low, and slowly bring the water to a simmer. Leave the pot to simmer for 2 hours, making sure it doesn't boil dry, then remove from the heat and discard any water remaining in the pot. Your pot is now ready to use. Alternatively, put the water-filled pot in a preheated 225°F oven and bake for 2 hours, then turn off the oven and leave the pot in the oven until the oven is cool. Use your clay pots often, and be gentle with them. Like all good things they won't last forever.

Chicken with Lily Buds and Dried Shiitake Mushrooms

—

This is a brothy, soothing cold-weather dish that is flavored mostly with ginger, rounded out with garlic and earthy dried shiitake mushrooms. It has the same appeal and wholesome flavor as chicken soup in the West, a classic comfort food. Accompany it with steamed rice to soak up the delicious sauce.

The chickens that you find at an Asian butcher shop are markedly different from your average supermarket bird. Most of them are spindly, bony critters, much smaller than their supermarket cousins, and because of that they're ideal for braising. For a full rundown of the different types of Asian chickens available, see page 101. If you don't have access to one of these Asian breeds, you'll get best results with this recipe if you use a free-range chicken, the kind that runs around and develops muscle, which makes for more flavorful meat.

- 3 pounds skin-on, bone-in whole chicken legs (separated into drumsticks and thighs), trimmed of excess fat
- 1 tablespoon rice wine (see page 215)
- 1 tablespoon cornstarch
- 1½ teaspoons kosher salt
- ¼ cup dried lily buds (see page 204)
- 12 dried shiitake mushrooms (see page 210)
- 6 cups chicken stock (see page 6)
- 3 tablespoons canola oil
- 2 by 1-inch piece fresh ginger, peeled and julienned
- 3 cloves garlic, crushed
- Fish sauce (see page 36), for seasoning
- Cilantro sprigs, for garnish (optional)

Serves 6 as a main course

1.
Put the chicken pieces in a shallow bowl, sprinkle with the rice wine, cornstarch, and salt, and turn the pieces to coat well. Cover and refrigerate for at least 2 hours or up to overnight. Bring to room temperature before browning.

2.
Put the shiitake mushrooms and lily buds in separate bowls, add hot water to cover to both bowls, and let soak for about 15 minutes, until softened. Drain the lily buds, trim away the tough end from each bud, and set aside. Drain the mushrooms, remove and discard the stems, cut each cap in half, and set aside.

3.
In a Dutch oven or other heavy-bottomed pot, heat the oil over medium-high heat. When the oil is hot, working in batches, add the chicken pieces and cook, turning once, for about 8 minutes, until browned on both sides. As each batch is ready, transfer it to a rimmed baking sheet.

4.
When all of the chicken has been browned, add 1 cup of stock to the now-empty pot and scrape the bottom of the pan with a wooden spoon to release the browned bits. Transfer to a clay pot and add the browned chicken along with the remaining chicken stock, ginger, garlic, lily buds, and mushrooms. Bring the liquid to a boil over medium heat, then lower the heat so the liquid is at a gentle simmer. Cook, uncovered, for about 25 minutes, until the chicken is opaque throughout and the sauce has reduced by about a third. Taste the sauce and adjust the seasoning by adding fish sauce, ½ teaspoon at a time.

5.
Garnish with cilantro and serve directly from the clay pot.

Chickens

—

Most of the chickens that make it to market in America are the same breed, a cross between a White Cornish and a White Plymouth Rock. They have large breasts and grow quickly, reaching maturity in a fraction of the time it takes other breeds. Unfortunately, these quick-growing birds also rarely wander outside or scratch in the dirt, so they don't build up flavorful muscle.

Given the uniformity of chickens from market to market, it's easy to forget that other breeds are available. In an Asian grocery store or butcher shop, you might find Brahma or Ac chickens, or birds labeled Loong Kong or Yellow Feather. Most eye-catching of all are the Silkies, which have black skin, bones, and flesh. They are frequently used for soups, and are purported to have medicinal properties.

These alternative breeds, often called heritage breeds, are generally much smaller than the standard grocery-store chicken, with a larger proportion of dark meat to light and a pronounced breastbone. They're often sold with their head and feet intact, but if you're squeamish, you can ask the butcher to remove them for you. Their meat tends to be tougher, making them the ideal chickens for soups and braised dishes.

If you don't have access to an Asian grocery store, it's worth seeking out pasture-raised heritage-breed chickens, which can be found at farmers' markets and some grocery stores. They'll have a more pronounced chicken flavor and a better texture, with more dark meat.

How to Chop a Whole Bird Asian-Style

Place the chicken breast-side up on a cutting board. With a cleaver, make a cut to separate the leg from the breast. Bend the leg backwards to reveal the joint and cut cleanly through it to separate the leg from the body. Repeat with the other leg. Remove the wings using the same method.

Separate the drumstick and thigh and, with swift cuts, chop each drumstick and thigh through the bone into three pieces. Cut off the wing tips and discard or save for stock. Cut through the keel bone, dividing the breast into two pieces. Cut each piece free from the backbone. Place the two breast halves on the cutting board and cut each lengthwise into two pieces, then crosswise through the bone into 1-inch pieces. Trim the rib cage from the backbone and discard, then cut the backbone into small pieces.

This method can be used with raw or cooked poultry.

Braising

Chicken Curry
—

Curry can be made in so many different styles, from the brothy coconut milk versions that are popular in Thailand to the thick, saucy Indian curries. The Vietnamese version is very brothy and rich, but contains no coconut milk. There are four components to curry: fat, sugar, acidity, and spice. The fat can come from coconut milk, animal fat, or oil, the sweetness from onions, carrots, or celery. The acidic element might be mango, tamarind, tomatoes, or citrus, and the spices vary from region to region. The best curries balance the four components.

Curry leaves and galangal (an aromatic root used throughout Thailand, Vietnam, and Indonesia) can be found at most well-stocked Asian groceries. When you see them, buy lots. Both will keep tightly sealed in plastic storage bags in the freezer for several months. If possible, salt the chicken the night before cooking so the meat is seasoned to the bone.

- 3 pounds skin-on, bone-in whole chicken legs (separated into drumsticks and thighs), trimmed of excess fat
- 1 teaspoon kosher salt
- ¼ cup plus 3 tablespoons canola oil
- 3 lemongrass stalks (see page 207)
- 2 yellow onions, diced (about 4 cups)
- 2 teaspoons shrimp paste (see page 215)
- 2 teaspoons minced garlic
- 1 teaspoon ground coriander
- 1 teaspoon ground turmeric
- ¼ teaspoon cayenne pepper
- ¼ teaspoon freshly ground black pepper
- 3 tablespoons rice wine (see page 215)
- ½ cup diced fresh or canned tomato
- 2 Thai chiles, stemmed and halved crosswise on the diagonal
- 6 fresh curry leaves (see page 204)
- 2 bay leaves
- 2 by 1-inch piece fresh galangal (see page 206), peeled and sliced
- 3 quarts chicken stock (see page 6)
- 3 carrots, peeled and cut crosswise into 1-inch pieces
- 2 medium Yukon gold potatoes, diced (about 1½ cups)

Serves 6 as a main course

1.
Put the chicken legs in a single layer on a rimmed baking sheet and season them on both sides with the salt. Cover loosely with plastic wrap and refrigerate overnight. The following day, bring the chicken to room temperature before cooking.

2.
In a Dutch oven or other heavy-bottomed pot, heat 3 tablespoons of the oil over medium-high heat. When the oil is hot, working in batches, add the chicken legs and cook, turning once, for about 8 minutes, until browned on both sides. As each batch is ready, transfer it to a clean rimmed baking sheet.

3.
Cut off the pale, fleshy part (the bottom 4 inches) of each lemongrass stalk and discard the dry tops. Crush the lemongrass with the side of a cleaver or a kitchen mallet, and set aside.

4.
In a large clay pot, heat the remaining ¼ cup oil over medium heat. Add the onions and cook, stirring occasionally, for about 25 minutes, until they are very soft and deep golden brown. If the onions begin to get too dark, lower the heat. Add the shrimp paste and garlic and cook for 1 minute. Stir in the coriander, turmeric, cayenne, and black pepper and cook for 1 minute longer.

5.
Stir in the wine and tomato and cook for 4 to 5 minutes, until the liquid has evaporated and the onion mixture looks dry. Add the chiles, curry and bay leaves, lemongrass, and galangal. Pour in the stock and bring the liquid to a boil. Lower the heat so the liquid is at a simmer and cook, uncovered, for 1½ hours, until the liquid is reduced by half.

6.
Pour the liquid through a fine-mesh sieve placed over a bowl. Remove the curry and bay leaves and the lemongrass stalks from the sieve and discard. Using a rubber spatula, press as much of the remaining onion mixture as possible through the sieve into the liquid.

7.
Return the strained braising liquid to the clay pot, place over medium heat, and bring to a boil. Add the browned chicken, carrot, and potato, lower the heat to a gentle simmer, and cook, uncovered, for 25 minutes, until the chicken is opaque throughout and the carrots and potatoes are tender.

8.
Remove from the heat and serve directly from the clay pot, accompanied by steamed rice or cooked rice vermicelli (see page 13).

Duck Legs with Bamboo, Virginia Ham, and Shiitake Mushrooms

—

China's Yunnan Province is justly famous for its ham, which boasts a good proportion of white fat to lean meat and adds a rich, smoky flavor to braises and stir-fries. It is not available in the States, but salt-cured, smoked southern country ham, like Smithfield ham from Virginia, is a decent substitute. The four ounces of ham used in this recipe may not seem like much, but it's the ingredient that adds the most body and flavor to the braising liquid, which has an earthy depth that enhances the flavor of the silky duck meat. Dried bamboo leaves and prepared bamboo shoots (or, if you're lucky, fresh ones) are available in Asian grocery stores. Although not essential, it is a good idea to make this braise a day ahead. Store the duck legs in the braising liquid and refrigerate; before reheating, remove any fat from the surface. Accompany with steamed rice for absorbing the rich braising liquid.

- 6 skin-on, bone-in duck legs, trimmed of excess fat
- 2 tablespoons kosher salt
- 20 dried shiitake mushrooms (see page 210)
- 2 tablespoons canola oil
- 4-ounce slice smoked country ham (such as Smithfield), cut into 4 equal pieces
- 2 cups diced yellow onions
- 3 dried bamboo leaves, rinsed
- 8 ounces fresh or prepared bamboo shoots (see page 105), sliced
- 7 cups chicken stock (see page 6)

Serves 6 as a main course

Note: Crispy Skin
Braising poultry with the skin on means that even if you have crisped the skin when you browned the pieces, it will invariably soften again during braising. But browning the duck legs before braising them is an important step because it helps render fat from the skin, making the finished braise less greasy. If you cannot stand the idea of soft skin (a texture appreciated in many Asian cuisines), when you remove the duck legs from the braising liquid, place them, skin side up, on a rimmed baking sheet and pat them dry with paper towels. Place the pan under the broiler 2 to 3 inches from the heating element until the skin crisps. It's not traditional, but it tastes good.

1.
Put the duck legs in a single layer on a rimmed baking sheet and season on both sides with the salt. Cover with plastic wrap and refrigerate overnight. The following day, rinse the legs under running cold water, then pat dry with a paper towel.

2.
In a bowl, combine the mushrooms with hot water to cover and let soak for about 15 minutes, until softened. Drain, and remove and discard the stems. Cut half of the mushroom caps (10) into quarters; leave the remaining mushroom caps whole.

3.
In a Dutch oven or other heavy-bottomed pot, heat the oil over medium heat. When the oil is hot, working in batches, add the duck legs skin side down and cook for about 8 to 10 minutes, until the skin is a deep golden brown and beginning to crisp. Flip the legs and cook for 3 minutes on the second side. As each batch is ready, transfer it to a clean rimmed baking sheet.

4.
After the last duck legs have been browned, pour all but 2 tablespoons of the fat in the pot into a small heatproof bowl (reserve for another use). Return the pan to the heat, add the ham and fry, turning once, for about 4 minutes, until browned on both sides. Transfer the ham to the baking sheet holding the duck legs. Add the onions to the fat remaining in the pot, decrease the heat to medium-low, and cook, stirring occasionally, for 20 to 25 minutes, until the onions are very soft and golden brown. Return the ham to the pot.

Fresh bamboo shoots, called *mang* in Vietnamese, are much better than canned, but they are difficult to find in the States. They have a crisp texture and a clean flavor that is irresistible. Fresh bamboo is grown around the world (including near Fremont, California, about forty miles southwest of San Francisco) and appears in Asian markets in the United States spring through early fall.

To prepare the fresh shoots for cooking, peel the tough outer leaves and trim the fibrous base, leaving a cone of tender, white flesh. Slice thinly lengthwise, and boil in salted water to cover for 20 to 30 minutes, until tender. This removes the toxic hydrocyanic acid naturally present in the shoot. Remove from the heat and let cool, then refrigerate in the cooking liquid in a tightly covered container. They will keep for up to a week.

When fresh bamboo is not in season–or if you cannot find it near you–vacuum-sealed (my preference) or canned shoots may be substituted. They are sold ready to use (no boiling required) and the best are white or very pale yellow. Unfortunately, most canned bamboo shoots have an unpleasant tinned flavor and fibrous texture. When using canned or vacuum-sealed bamboo shoots, slice them first, then rinse them thoroughly under cold running water to remove any off flavor and any white residue that has accumulated in their ridges.

Braising

5.
Arrange 3 duck legs in a single layer on top of the onions and ham in the pot. Top with 2 bamboo leaves, followed by a second single layer of 3 legs, and then the third bamboo leaf. Top with the whole shiitakes and pour in the stock. Bring the liquid to a boil over medium heat, then decrease the heat so the liquid is at a gentle simmer. Cover and cook for about 1¼ hours, until the meat is tender but not falling off the bone. Check periodically to ensure the liquid is not simmering too vigorously.

6.
Remove from the heat. Transfer the duck legs to a plate and set aside. Remove and discard the bamboo leaves and pour the liquid through a fine-mesh sieve placed over a bowl. Discard the ham pieces and using a rubber spatula, press against the contents of the sieve to force as much liquid as possible through the sieve.

7.
Return the duck legs to the pot and pour the strained liquid over them. Add the quartered mushrooms and the bamboo slices and bring to a boil over medium heat. Decrease the heat so the liquid is at gentle simmer and cook, uncovered, for 15 minutes.

8.
Remove from the heat. Using a metal spoon, skim the fat from the surface. Serve directly from the clay pot.

Soy-Braised Pork Belly with Ginger and Star Anise

—

My Aunt, Ah Nueng, is the best cook in our family and taught me how to make this classic Cantonese dish. The multistep process is time-consuming, but worth the effort. Blanching draws out impurities and softens the pork skin, the frying step helps render excess fat, and the final soaking makes the belly easy to cut into thin strips. When buying pork belly, look for "five story" pork, with five alternating layers of fat and meat. The pork gets even better if it sits in the braising liquid for a day, so don't be afraid to make this ahead. Any leftover meat makes an excellent filling for steamed buns (page 83). Serve the pork with steamed rice to absorb the cooking juices.

- 2 pounds skin-on pork belly, in one piece
- 3 tablespoons dark soy sauce (see page 215)
- 1 cup canola oil
- 1½ cubes fermented red bean curd (see page 206), mashed (about 1 tablespoon)
- 1½ tablespoons oyster sauce (see page 214)
- 2 teaspoons sugar
- 4 whole star anise pods (see page 211)
- 2 cloves garlic, crushed
- 4 silver-dollar-size slices fresh ginger
- 6 scallions, cut into 3-inch lengths
- 1½ cups pickled mustard greens, homemade (see page 119) or store-bought, rinsed and coarsely chopped

Serves 6 as part of a multicourse meal

1.
Bring a large pot of water to a boil. Add the pork belly and cook for about 5 minutes, until the water returns to a boil. Drain the pork and, when cool enough to handle, prick holes all over the skin using a fork or a pronged tenderizer. Rub the skin side with 1 tablespoon of the soy sauce.

2.
In a large, deep Dutch oven or heavy-bottomed pot, heat the oil over medium-high heat. When the oil is hot but not smoking, add the pork belly, skin side down. Decrease the heat to medium, cover the pot partially to protect yourself from oil splatters, and cook for about 10 minutes, until the skin is golden brown and crisp. Carefully flip the pork over and cook for an additional 3 minutes on the second side. Remove the pot from the heat, transfer the pork to a bowl, and pour the fat that has accumulated in the pot into a small heatproof bowl. Set the fat aside.

3.
Add cold water to cover the pork and let stand for 30 minutes. The skin will bubble up and soften. Remove the pork from the bowl, discard the water, and cut the meat crosswise into ¼-inch-wide strips.

4.
While the pork is soaking, make the sauce. In a small bowl, combine the bean curd, oyster sauce, the remaining 2 tablespoons soy, and the sugar. Mash the bean curd with the back of a spoon, then stir until the sauce is smooth. Add the star anise and stir to combine.

5.
In a large clay pot or heavy-bottomed pot, heat 2 tablespoons of the reserved fat over medium heat. Add the garlic and cook, stirring, for about 30 seconds, until fragrant. Add the ginger, scallions, and sauce mixture and cook for 2 minutes more.

6.
Add the pork strips, stir to coat with the sauce, then add 3 cups water and mix well. Bring to a boil and decrease the heat so the mixture is simmering gently. Cover and simmer for 1 hour. At the 1 hour mark, stir in the mustard greens, re-cover, and cook for 15 minutes longer, until both meat and fat are very tender.

7.
Remove from the heat and serve the pork directly from the clay pot, accompanied by steamed white rice.

Catfish Clay Pot

—

Catfish is widely available and commonly eaten in Vietnam. Although some people object to what they describe as the muddy flavor of this freshwater fish, others cannot get enough of this classic southern Vietnamese clay pot, including one regular customer at The Slanted Door who orders this dish for dessert, often after having already eaten one as his main course. In Vietnam, catfish are typically butchered into steaks, not fillets, which is what you see most often in America. Bone-in steaks work best for this recipe, so you can either buy a whole cleaned fish and cut it up yourself, or ask the fishmonger to do it. Steamed rice is nice for soaking up the sauce.

- 2 pounds catfish steaks, each about 1 inch thick
- ½ teaspoon freshly ground black pepper
- 1¼ cups caramel sauce (see page 109)
- ¼ cup chicken stock (see page 6)
- 2 Thai chiles, stemmed and halved on the diagonal
- 10 strands finely julienned fresh ginger
- 4 cilantro sprigs, for garnish (optional)

Serves 6 as part of a multicourse meal

1.
Season the catfish steaks with black pepper and put them in a clay pot, saucepan, or high-sided frying pan large enough to accommodate them snugly in a single layer. Add the caramel sauce, stock, chiles, and ginger.

2.
Place over medium heat and bring to a boil. Decrease the heat so the liquid is at a simmer, cover partially, and cook for 6 minutes. Gently flip the catfish pieces, re-cover partially, and continue cooking for 6 minutes longer, until the flesh is beginning to pull away from the bone.

3.
Garnish with the cilantro and serve immediately directly from the pot. If using a saucepan or frying pan, transfer to a platter, garnish with the cilantro, and serve.

Caramel Sauce

—

If you're familiar with French food, you know all about the mother sauces, the building blocks of classical French cuisine. In Vietnam, caramel sauce plays the same role. I don't want to overstate the importance of this recipe, but this combination of water, sugar, and fish sauce is so good, so right, and such an integral part of so many Vietnamese dishes, from Caramelized Lemongrass Shrimp (page 116) to Pork Claypot with Young Coconut Juice (page 110), that you need to make a batch right away. Sugar and fish sauce are used with abandon in the food of Vietnam. The sugar balances the funk of the fish sauce, and the fish sauce tempers the cloying character of the sugar.

As the story goes, there was once a young academic who came from a poor family but desperately wanted to go to university in the city. He had no money, but he set out on his journey with a bottle of caramel sauce. He was too poor to afford meat, but he didn't want to give himself away as a broke bumpkin, so he carved a fish out of wood and at every meal he would pour the caramel sauce over the wooden fish and some rice and then pretend to eat the fish. What's the moral here? Well, obviously it's that the sauce, not the fish, is the most important element. Or, alternatively, that the sauce is so good that it has the power to transform a wooden fish. Either way, you should have this in your pantry at all times. You can make a large batch because it keeps well, unrefrigerated, for a few months. That way, you're more likely to have it on hand for making any one of the dozens of Vietnamese recipes that call for a small amount.

Although you can make caramel sauce with white sugar, which you must slowly caramelize before adding the fish sauce, I use light brown palm sugar, which is available in Asian markets (see page 208, for more information). Starting with palm sugar makes the process go a bit faster, and there is less of a threat of taking a white-sugar caramel too far and ending up with a scorched mess. This recipe can be halved easily.

- 2 pounds light brown palm sugar (see page 208), chopped into pieces
- 2½ cups fish sauce

Makes about 4 cups

1.
In a heavy-bottomed 4-quart pot, gently melt the sugar over medium-low heat, stirring frequently. This will take 10 to 12 minutes. Do not be tempted to rush the process or you may scorch the sugar.

2.
When the sugar is lump free, completely melted, and just beginning to boil, remove the pan from the heat and very slowly pour in the fish sauce while stirring constantly. Be careful, as it will bubble furiously. Use the sauce right away, or let cool completely, transfer to an airtight container, and store in a cool cupboard for up to 3 months.

Braising

Pork Clay Pot with Young Coconut Juice

—

I had this dish the first time I went back to Vietnam in 1992 after a seventeen-year hiatus. My hometown, Đà Lat, is about an eight-hour drive from Ho Chi Minh City. You pass through a mountain town on the way, and everyone stops at the rest stop there for fuel and food. That's where I first tasted this dish—rest-stop food, Vietnamese style. I had no idea that coconut could be so delicate. Using the water (instead of the high-fat milk often used in curries, which is pressed from coconut flesh) gives the dish a light, tropical flavor with a subtle coconut accent, a perfect foil to the rich pork. If you can't find whole young coconuts, you can use canned coconut water (not milk!) with good results. Serve this dish with steamed rice.

- 2 young coconuts, or 3 cups canned coconut water
- 1½ pounds meaty pork ribs, cut crosswise through the bone into 2-inch pieces (ask your butcher to do this)
- 1½ pounds boneless pork shoulder, cut into 1¼-inch cubes
- ¾ teaspoon kosher salt
- 1 teaspoon freshly ground black pepper
- 3 to 4 tablespoons canola oil
- 2 large shallots, sliced into ⅛-inch-thick rings
- 2 large cloves garlic, crushed
- 2 Thai chiles, stemmed and crushed
- 3 by 2-inch piece fresh ginger, peeled and finely julienned
- 1 cup caramel sauce (see page 109)
- 1 cup pork stock (see page 5) or water
- 6 hard-boiled eggs, peeled

Serves 6 as part of a multicourse meal

1.

If using young coconuts, here is how to extract the water: With the back edge of a cleaver (the corner of the blade closest to the handle), cut a 2-inch hole in the top of each coconut. Drain the liquid from each coconut through a fine-mesh sieve into a large measuring pitcher. You should have 3 cups. If you have less, add water as needed to reach that amount.

2.

With a heavy knife or cleaver, split each coconut in half lengthwise. Using a small spoon, gently scrape out the soft, white flesh from the interior. Cut the flesh into 2 by ½-inch strips and set aside. If using canned coconut water, omit this ingredient.

3.

Season the meat with salt and half of the pepper. In a Dutch oven or heavy-bottomed pot, heat 3 tablespoons of the oil over medium-high heat. When the oil is hot, working in batches, add the pork ribs and pork shoulder and cook, turning as needed, for about 8 minutes, until browned on all sides. As each batch is ready, transfer it to a rimmed baking sheet or plate. If necessary to prevent scorching, add the remaining 1 tablespoon oil.

4.

Pour off all but 2 tablespoons of the fat in the pot. Add the shallots to the now-empty pot, decrease the heat to medium, and cook, stirring, for about 3 minutes, until softened. Add the garlic, chiles, and ginger and cook for 3 minutes longer. Remove from the heat.

5.

Transfer the shallot mixture to a large clay pot, then add the browned meat and season with remaining ½ teaspoon pepper. Add the caramel sauce, stock, and coconut water. The liquid should almost, but not completely, cover the meat; add more water as needed. Bring the liquid to a boil over medium heat, decrease the heat to a simmer, cover, and cook at a vigorous simmer for about 50 minutes, until the meat is tender but not falling off the bone.

6.

Add the eggs and coconut flesh, re-cover, and cook for 5 minutes longer, just until the eggs absorb some of the color and flavor of the caramel sauce. Be careful not to overcook them. Serve the pork and eggs directly from the clay pot.

Lo Soi Braised Pork

—

Lo soi, literally "old water" in Chinese, is a classic preparation for duck, chicken, and pork that is commonly eaten in Hong Kong. The braising liquid, also known as a mother sauce or master sauce, can—and should—be saved and used again and again as it gets better with each use. Some chefs have been known to use the same *lo soi* for their entire career, much like bakers use the same sourdough starter or Japanese yakitori chefs use the same sauce for years, adding to it as needed. We use it in our wonton soup, but it's good on its own, sliced and served with rice and greens.

- 3-inch piece Chinese cinnamon (see page 203)
- 3 whole star anise pods (see page 211)
- 10 whole cloves
- 1 black cardamom pod (see page 203)
- 2 by 1-inch piece fresh ginger, crushed
- ½ teaspoon five-spice powder (see page 205)
- 2 tablespoons fish sauce (see page 36)
- 2 cups light soy sauce (see page 215)
- 8 ounces light brown palm sugar (see page 208), or 2 tablespoons light brown sugar
- 1 pound lean pork shoulder, cut in 2 uniform pieces

Serves 6 as part of a multicourse meal

1.
In a dry frying pan, toast the cinnamon, star anise, and cloves over medium-high heat for about 30 seconds, until fragrant. Transfer to a large stockpot and add the cardamom, ginger, five-spice powder, fish sauce, soy sauce, and sugar. Add 7 cups water and bring to a boil over high heat, stirring occasionally.

2.
Lower the heat so the liquid is at a steady simmer, add the pork, and simmer for 20 minutes. Remove the pot from the heat and let the pork sit in the liquid for 30 minutes.

3.
Remove the pork from the liquid and let cool completely before slicing, or wrap tightly and refrigerate for up to 2 days before using. Skim off any scum from the surface of the liquid, then strain through a fine-mesh sieve into a storage container, discarding the solids. Let cool completely, then cover tightly and refrigerate until you are ready to use it again. If you do not use the liquid at least once a month, return it to a pot, bring it to a rolling boil, and boil hard for 5 minutes, then allow it to return to room temperature before refrigerating again. If you do this consistently, the liquid will keep for up to a year. The liquid can also be frozen; after thawing, reheat and taste, adding more water or stock if it's too salty.

4.
Each time you use the liquid to cook something, add fresh spices (cinnamon, star anise, cloves, cardamom, and ginger) and taste and adjust the flavor by adding more soy sauce or sugar to taste.

Variation:
Lo soi is commonly used as a braising liquid for whole ducks and chickens. If you want to try it, double the recipe (including the water), add the duck or chicken in place of the pork, and simmer for about 45 minutes for a whole 5-pound duck and 35 minutes for a whole 3-pound chicken, or until almost cooked through. Remove from heat and let the duck or chicken sit in the liquid 30 minutes before serving.

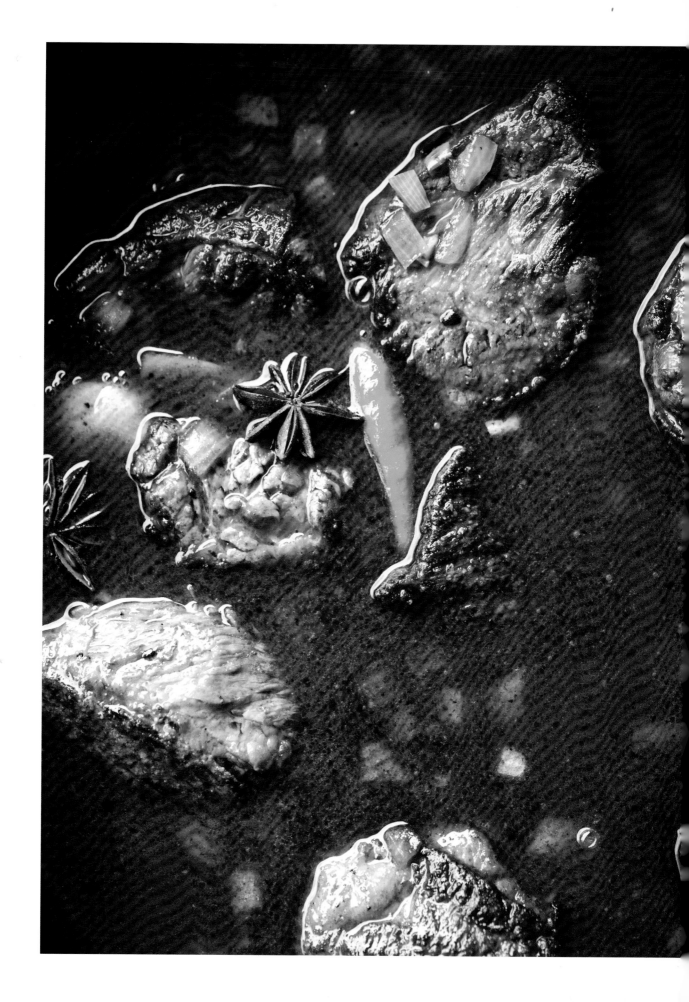

Lemongrass Beef Stew

—

Obviously this dish is imported from France, but it has a very Vietnamese sensibility, seasoned with lemongrass, ginger, Thai chile and fish sauce. You can make the stew with beef chuck or brisket, but I like to use boneless short ribs. Once an overlooked cut of meat, short ribs are now on menus across the country (and, sadly, are no longer as cheap as they once were). The meat is generously marbled with fat, which breaks down during the braising process, yielding a velvety sauce and extremely tender texture.

This stew is brothier and more soup-like than Western versions, and I often serve it over rice noodles. But if you prefer a thicker sauce, you can remove the meat and vegetables at the end and boil the sauce over high heat until it has reduced and thickened to your desired consistency, then serve it with bowls of steamed rice or with a chunk of baguette.

- 3 pounds boneless beef short ribs, cut into 1½-inch cubes
- 4 tablespoons canola oil
- 1 teaspoon kosher salt
- ½ teaspoon freshly ground black pepper
- 2 cups diced yellow onions
- 2 teaspoons minced garlic
- ¼ cup finely minced lemongrass (see page 207)
- 3 tablespoons tomato paste
- 2 by 1-inch piece fresh ginger, peeled and smashed
- 2 whole star anise pods (see page 211)
- 1 or 2 Thai chiles, stemmed, plus 1 teaspoon minced, for garnish
- 6 cups beef stock (see page 7)
- 3 carrots, peeled and cut into 2-inch lengths
- 8 ounces daikon radish, peeled and cut into 1-inch lengths
- About 2 tablespoons fish sauce (see page 36)
- ¼ cup finely sliced fresh Thai basil (see page 213), for garnish

Serves 6 as a main course

1.
Place the beef in a bowl. Drizzle with 1 tablespoon of the oil, sprinkle with the salt and pepper, and stir to coat. Let stand while you prepare all of the other ingredients.

2.
In a large Dutch oven or heavy-bottomed pot, heat the remaining 3 tablespoons oil over high heat. When the oil is hot, working in batches, add the beef and cook, turning as needed, for about 8 minutes, until browned on all sides. As each batch is ready, transfer it to a rimmed baking sheet.

3.
Decrease the heat to medium and add the onion to the now-empty pot. Cook, stirring frequently, for about 10 minutes, until the onion is a deep golden brown. Stir in the garlic and cook, stirring, for 30 seconds more. Add the lemongrass, tomato paste, ginger, star anise, and whole chile to taste and stir to combine. Transfer the mixture to a large clay pot.

4.
Add the beef and any accumulated juices to the clay pot and pour in the stock. Bring the liquid to a boil over medium heat, decrease the heat so the liquid is at a gentle simmer, cover, and cook, stirring occasionally, for 1½ hours, until the meat is just tender.

5.
Add the carrots and daikon, re-cover, and cook for 30 minutes longer, until the vegetables are cooked through and the meat is very tender. Remove from the heat and stir in the fish sauce, 1 tablespoon at a time, to taste.

6.
Serve the stew directly from the clay pot. Top each serving with some of the basil and minced chile.

Caramelized Lemongrass Shrimp

—

If you have homemade caramel sauce and roasted chile paste on hand, you can have this incredibly satisfying dish on the table in 15 minutes. You may be tempted to use peeled, headless shrimp for this recipe. They will work, and the dish will taste good, but it won't be as delicious as it will be if you use head-on shrimp. The heads impart a richness to the sauce. My nine-year-old son actually prefers the heads to the bodies, and makes a big show of sucking each head to remove all of the meat and flavor. We buy shrimp from the Louisiana Gulf, where many of the shrimpers are of Vietnamese descent. They are worth seeking out and paying more for.

- 2 pounds medium head-on shrimp in their shells, preferably from the Louisiana Gulf
- ¼ teaspoon freshly ground black pepper
- 2 tablespoons canola oil
- 2 shallots, thinly sliced into rings
- 2 Thai chiles, stemmed and halved on the diagonal
- ¼ cup finely minced lemongrass (see page 207)
- 1 teaspoon minced garlic
- 2 by 1-inch piece fresh ginger, peeled and finely julienned
- 1 tablespoon plus 2 teaspoons roasted chile paste (see page 117)
- ½ cup caramel sauce (see page 109)
- ¼ cup chicken stock (see page 6) or water

Serves 6 as part of a multicourse meal

1.
To prepare the shrimp, using scissors, remove the sharp spike at the tail of each shrimp and the spike in the center of the head. Cut off the eyes and discard, then separate the head from the body and reserve the head. Peel each shrimp body, removing the tail segments, then devein. Sprinkle bodies with the pepper and set aside.

2.
In a 2-quart clay pot or high-sided sauté pan, heat the oil over medium heat. Add the shallots, chiles, and reserved shrimp heads and cook, stirring, for about 30 seconds, until fragrant. Add the lemongrass, garlic, ginger, and chile paste and cook, stirring, for 1 minute more. Pour in the caramel sauce and stock and stir to combine.

3.
Add the shrimp bodies to the pot and toss to coat with the aromatic ingredients. Increase the heat to medium-high and cook, stirring occasionally, for about 6 minutes total, until shrimp are bright pink.

4.
Serve directly from the clay pot, accompanied by steamed white rice.

Roasted Chile Paste

—

Our roasted chile paste runs circles around store-bought versions. The Sichuan peppercorns give it an almost floral, complicated heat, punched up by red pepper flakes and mellowed out by the ground bean paste. It's used as a condiment, added to dipping sauces, and used as an ingredient in cooked dishes. If you are opting for store-bought, you'll find it in glass or plastic jars, often labeled chile-bean or saté paste (see bean paste page 214). Look for a brand made without preservatives.

- 1 tablespoon Sichuan peppercorns (see page 211)
- 1 tablespoon annatto seeds (see page 202)
- ½ cup finely chopped shallots
- ½ cup canola oil
- ¼ cup finely minced garlic (about 8 cloves)
- ¼ cup red pepper flakes
- ⅓ cup ground bean paste (see page 214)
- 2 tablespoons rice wine (see page 215)
- 2 tablespoons sugar
- 2 tablespoons light soy sauce (see page 215)

Makes about 1⅛ cups

1.
Combine the peppercorns and annatto seeds in a spice grinder (or use a mortar and pestle) and grind coarsely. Set aside.

2.
In a small saucepan, combine the shallots and oil over medium heat and cook, stirring frequently, for about 6 minutes, until the shallots are light gold. Add the garlic and cook, stirring frequently, for about 4 minutes longer, until the garlic and shallot are lightly browned.

3.
Stir in the red pepper flakes and the peppercorn-annatto mixture, mixing well. Add the wine, sugar, and soy sauce and continue cooking, stirring, for 1 minute longer. Remove from the heat and let cool completely. Use immediately, or transfer to an airtight container and refrigerate for up to 3 months.

How to Chop Lemongrass

The texture of chopped lemongrass is important. We go through cases and cases of lemongrass each week for the restaurants, so hand-chopping is not possible. But at home it's always my first choice.

First, cut the bottom ½-inch off each lemongrass stalk and trim the greenish, woody top portion and discard. Peel the outer layers from the stalk until you arrive at the firm, tender center. With a sharp knife, thinly slice the stalk into coins, then run your knife through the pile of coins until you have reduced them to nubby bits. You want to detect the bits of lemongrass in a finished dish: they should register on your tongue, then dissolve, leaving only the bright aroma behind.

To preserve the aromatic quality of fresh lemongrass, chop it just before using. If you live in a place where lemongrass is hard to come by, buy extra: whole stalks can be frozen for future use.

Braised Branzino with Tomatoes and Pickled Mustard Greens

—

There's an expression in Vietnamese that says if you don't know how to eat a whole fish, you have a dumb tongue—too dumb to sort out the bones from the delicate flesh. When choosing fish, go by smell—a new fish should smell like a new iPod. In other words, it shouldn't smell like anything. It definitely should not smell fishy (and yes, you can ask your fishmonger to let you smell it), and the eyes should be clear. As a concession to those who can't stand having their dinner look them in the eye, I've included a variation that uses fillets. But I'd like you to try the whole fish version at least once in your life. At The Slanted Door, we like to use Early Girl tomatoes, which are on the small side and have a concentrated tomato flavor, for this recipe. If you can't find them, use the best firm, yet ripe, tomatoes you can find.

- 1 (1½- to 2-pound) whole branzino, cleaned with head and tail intact
- 1 teaspoon kosher salt
- ½ teaspoon freshly ground black pepper
- ¼ cup all-purpose flour
- 4 tablespoons canola oil
- 1 large shallot, thinly sliced into rings
- 8 scallions, white and light green parts only, thinly sliced
- 2 teaspoons minced garlic
- 2 Thai chiles, stemmed and crushed
- 2 tomatoes (such as Early Girl or Roma), cored and quartered through the stem end
- ¼ cup coarsely chopped pickled mustard greens, homemade (see opposite) or store-bought
- 2 cups chicken stock (see page 6)
- 1 teaspoon fish sauce (see page 36)
- ¼ cup chopped fresh cilantro, for garnish

Serves 3 to 4 as part of a multicourse meal

1.
Rinse the fish, pat dry, and transfer to a cutting board. With a sharp knife, slash the fish on the diagonal 3 or 4 times on each side, cutting all the way to the bone. Season the fish on both sides and inside the cavity with the salt and pepper, then dust both sides with the flour, brushing off the excess.

2.
In a 12-inch nonstick skillet, heat 3 tablespoons of the oil over high heat. When oil is hot, add the fish and cook until well-browned on one side, about 5 minutes. Flip and cook on the second side 5 minutes more. Transfer to a rimmed baking sheet.

3.
Heat the remaining 1 tablespoon oil in the now-empty pan over medium heat. (If using a clay pot, do this step and all of the remaining steps in it instead of the pan.) Add the shallot and scallions and cook, stirring, for about 3 minutes, until softened. Add the garlic and chiles and cook, stirring, for about 1 minute longer, until fragrant but not browned.

4.
Add the tomatoes and cook for about 5 minutes, until the tomato pieces begin to soften and release their juices. Add the mustard greens and stir to combine, then pour in the stock. Gently slide the fish into the liquid, increase the heat to medium-high, and cook, basting with the hot liquid, for about 8 minutes, until the fish is just cooked through. Use the tip of a knife to check; the flesh should flake easily.

5.
Stir in the fish sauce, transfer to a serving platter, and garnish with the cilantro.

Pickled Mustard Greens

—

Mustard greens, also known as mustard cabbage and by its Cantonese name, *gai choy*, have deep green, ruffly leaves and long, wide stalks. They are sold in bunches at most Asian markets; look for bunches with firm stalks and without any yellowing. The greens can be spicy, but take especially well to pickling. Pickled mustard greens are typically paired with rich foods, where they provide great contrast (page 106), and are also frequently used in seafood dishes.

- 1½ cups distilled white vinegar
- 1 cup sugar
- ¼ cup coarse kosher salt
- 2 pounds mustard greens (*gai choy*), chopped into 3-inch lengths

Makes about 6 cups

1.
To make the pickling liquid, in a saucepan, bring 2¼ cups water to a boil over high heat. Decrease the heat to low and add the vinegar, sugar and salt. Cook, stirring occasionally, until the sugar, and salt have dissolved. Remove from the heat and let cool to room temperature.

2.
Bring a large pot filled with water to a boil. Add the greens and cook for about 3 minutes, until crisp tender. Drain well, then spread the heads and leaves on kitchen towels and let cool completely to room temperature.

3.
Transfer the greens to a nonreactive airtight container and pour the cooled pickling liquid over the top. The greens should be fully immersed in the liquid. If they are not, move them to a different vessel in which they will be fully immersed. Cover and let stand at room temperature for 2 days before using. The mustard greens will keep in a tightly capped container in the refrigerator for up to 2 months.

Variation: Fillet
If you prefer not to cook a whole fish, this recipe works equally well with skinless halibut or black cod (sablefish) fillets (a 6-ounce portion per serving is about the right size). Unlike the whole fish, the fillets do not need to be browned. Season them with salt and pepper and set aside. Begin with step 3 of the recipe, adding the fillets as instructed in step 4. Once the fillets have been added to the liquid, check them for doneness frequently as the exact cooking time will depend on their size and thickness.

Yuba Dumplings with Miso Broth
—

Yuba, the Japanese term for bean curd sheets, are the protein-rich "skins" that are generated when heating soy milk in making tofu. We get our handmade *yuba* from Hodo Soy Beanery, a Bay Area company owned by Vietnam-born Minh Tsai, where it is made fresh each week. A classic ingredient in Buddhist cuisine, it can be thinly sliced and stir-fried, used as a wrapper, or dressed and eaten as a cold salad. If you can't find fresh *yuba*, dried *yuba* can be substituted, though the flavor and texture pale in comparison.

Although this recipe isn't difficult, it does require a lot of chopping, which takes time, so plan to make it when you don't mind hanging out in the kitchen for a few hours or you have a few willing assistants.

Filling
- 1 cup dried shiitake mushrooms (see page 210)
- 1 (2-ounce) package cellophane noodles (see page 12)
- 2 tablespoons rice wine (see page 215)
- 2 tablespoons vegetarian stir-fry sauce (see page 215)
- 1 tablespoon light soy sauce (see page 215)
- 1 teaspoon toasted sesame oil
- 2 tablespoons canola oil
- 1 cup minced shallots (about 3 extra-large shallots)
- ¼ teaspoon kosher salt
- ½ teaspoon minced garlic
- 2 cups fresh shiitake mushrooms (about 5 ounces), stemmed and finely chopped
- 1 cup finely diced fresh water chestnuts (see page 213) or jicama (see page 206)
- 2 pressed tofu cakes (see page 209), about 5 ounces total, finely diced
- Pinch of ground white pepper
- ¾ cup chopped scallions, white and light green parts only

- 1 pound fresh or dried yuba (bean curd) sheets (see page 213)
- 5 tablespoons light yellow miso
- 2 silver-dollar-size slices fresh ginger, each about ¼ inch thick
- Scallion oil (see below), for garnish

Makes 18 dumplings; serves 6 as an appetizer

Scallion Oil
—

This simple condiment adds sweetness and richness to dishes, as well as a mild onion flavor. When you pour the hot oil over the scallion slices it should sizzle vigorously, parcooking the scallions and extracting their flavor.

- 1 cup thinly sliced scallions, green part only
- 1 teaspoon sugar
- 1 teaspoon kosher salt
- ¼ cup canola oil

In a heatproof bowl, combine the scallions, sugar, and salt. In a small saucepan, heat the oil over medium heat until shimmering but not smoking. Pour the oil over the scallions; it will sizzle vigorously. Stir gently, then let cool. If not using right away, cover and refrigerate. The oil will keep for up to 1 day.

1.

To make the filling, place the dried shiitakes in a bowl, add hot water to cover, and let stand for 15 minutes, until softened. Drain, remove and discard the stems, and squeeze the caps dry. Finely chop the caps and set aside.

2.

Place the cellophane noodles in a bowl, add very hot water to cover, and let stand for 10 to 15 minutes, until softened. Drain and set aside.

3.

In a small bowl, stir together the wine, stir-fry sauce, soy sauce, and sesame oil. Set aside.

4.

In a large nonstick frying pan, heat the canola oil over medium heat. Add the shallots, sprinkle with the salt, and cook, stirring frequently, for about 6 minutes, until softened. Add the garlic and cook, stirring, for 30 seconds, then stir in all of the mushrooms (both fresh and dried), the water chestnuts, and the tofu. Cook, stirring frequently, for 5 minutes longer.

5.

Gently stir in the noodles, add the wine mixture, and toss gently to combine all of the ingredients. Season with the pepper and stir in the scallions. Remove from the heat and set the filling aside to cool.

6.

If using dried yuba sheets, soak them in warm water to cover for about 5 to 10 minutes, until softened. Remove from the water and pat dry. If using fresh sheets, unwrap them and carefully separate them. Cut the sheets into 5-inch squares.

7.

To form each dumpling, place a yuba square on a work surface, positioning it so that you are facing a diamond shape. Put ¼ cup of the filling in the lower one-third of the wrapper, using your fingers to shape the filling into a rectangle and leaving 1 inch of the wrapper uncovered at either end of the filling and the point uncovered. Bring the point nearest to you up and over the filling, then roll the filling a single turn away from you to enclose it. Fold in the sides of the wrapper (it will now resemble an open envelope). Continue rolling tightly until the top point is folded over the filling and the finished cylinder resembles a spring roll. Repeat with the remaining squares and filling.

8.

Transfer the dumplings, seam side down, to a 12-inch frying pan, crowding them together. In a large measuring pitcher or a small bowl, whisk together the miso and 3 cups warm water until the miso has dissolved. Taste the mixture. The flavor of miso varies from brand to brand; you may need to add more miso to achieve a flavorful broth.

9.

Pour the miso broth over the dumplings, then add the coins of ginger to the pan. Place over medium-high heat and heat for about 9 minutes, until the broth is bubbling and the dumplings are heated through.

10.

Serve the dumplings immediately, in shallow individual bowls, accompanied with some of the broth. Garnish each serving with a drizzle of scallion oil.

The other techniques featured in this book—steaming, braising, grilling, frying—are used throughout the world. But stir-frying, specifically in a wok, is unique to Asian cuisine, and in China, where it originated and where most homes still don't have ovens, it remains the primary cooking method. Chinese immigrants

introduced the technique to Vietnam—and elsewhere throughout Asia—where it was quickly adopted.

Wok is the Cantonese word for "pot," and this style of cooking probably began out of necessity. Cooking food quickly over high heat is perfect for fuel-poor areas, such as much of rural China and Vietnam where gas, wood, and propane are in short supply.

A round-bottomed wok, made of spun steel or cast iron, makes the most of a small, hot fire: it transfers heat well, and the cooking surface is relatively large. Cutting the ingredients into small pieces serves two purposes: they cook quickly and they're easy to pick up and eat with chopsticks.

Every Chinese restaurant in America offers wok-cooked dishes, but the technique still seems exotic to most Western cooks. This probably has something to do with the perception that wok cooking requires the ferocious heat of a professional stove. But it's entirely

possible to make good stir-fried dishes at home, even without a wok.

The biggest roadblock for a Western cook attempting to stir-fry at home is not the stove (though electric stoves do make it more difficult). It's lack of patience. A wok is not a salad bowl with a heat source under it. You can't just dump everything into it at once and hope for the best. Ingredients have to be carefully cut and prepared, added in a particular order, and attentively tended to during the (brief) cooking time. Because most home stoves don't get as hot as restaurant stoves, at home it is best to cook batches of a single dish. Otherwise, you'll end up with a soggy mess. For that reason, the recipes in this chapter serve two or three people as part of a multicourse meal. If you have more diners at your table, cook a second batch rather than doubling the recipe.

Stir-frying is high-heat cooking. You have to let the pan get very hot before you

start adding your ingredients. On a home stove, this means setting the wok on the burner that burns hottest, turning up the heat all the way, and waiting. How long to wait? That'll depend on your stove and your wok, but if you're using a spun-steel wok (see my recommendations on how to choose a wok, page 126), the metal should take on a matte appearance and a drop or two of water flicked onto the surface should evaporate immediately on contact.

Before you begin cooking, make sure all of your ingredients are ready and within arms reach. Once you start, things happen quickly. If I'm stir-frying heartier vegetables, like Chinese broccoli, I blanch them first in the wok in boiling water, then set them  aside. Often, I'll partially cook meat and fish briefly in hot oil. Both of these steps give you a head start on the wok cooking, which is especially useful when you're cooking on a home stove. Of course, a wok is not essential to making a good stir-fry. You can get decent results with a hot sauté pan, too.

Above all else, the key ingredient to cooking successfully in a wok is honing your instincts. For many Western cooks, the wok is an unfamiliar pot and stir-frying is a new style of cooking: both take some getting used to. The best way to become familiar with wok cooking is to cook in your wok on your home stove. Developing the necessary instincts requires time and practice. But you'll soon figure out how long it takes for your wok to get hot, when to add each ingredient, and when to pull the finished stir-fry from the heat. As you become more familiar with using a wok, and as your wok's nonstick patina develops with age and use, you'll probably find yourself turning to stir-frying often— not so exotic or impossible after all.

How to Choose a Wok

—

First, don't bother with a nonstick wok. You want a surface that is friendly to oil, not one that repels it. For home use, I like spun-steel woks, which are cheap and easy to find. Cast-iron woks are good for deep-frying but are too heavy for stir-frying. Stainless-steel woks are too light and prone to hot spots. If you have a gas stove, get a round-bottomed wok; if you're working with an electric stove, you're going to need a flat-bottomed wok.

I like a fourteen-inch-diameter wok. It gives you the space to toss food around (the "stir" in stir-fry) without it slopping over the rim and onto the floor. It is a good size for deep-frying, too. Woks that have a wooden arm and a metal or wooden loop opposite are the easiest ones to maneuver, as opposed to woks with two metal loops opposite each other, or a wooden handle and no loop.

If you are purchasing a round-bottomed wok, buy a wok ring, too. It stabilizes the wok on the stove top and keeps it as close as possible to the heat source. Get a wok ring that is large enough to fit over your burner with the grate removed. You might also want to pick up a wok spatula, which is a shovel-shaped, long-armed metal spatula that is well-suited to the contours of a round-bottomed wok.

How to Clean and Season a New Wok
—

A new spun-steel wok will come coated in a thin layer of manufacturing grease. Before you cook anything in your wok, you'll need to remove that grease and start the seasoning process, which is not unlike what you do to get a cast-iron frying pan ready to use.

When you get your new wok home, scrub it vigorously with a stainless-steel scouring pad and hot, soapy water. This is the only time in the life of your wok that it should be cleaned with soap. Dry the wok with paper towels.

The most effective way to remove all of that manufacturing grease and prepare the pan to absorb oil—which will eventually give it its nonstick patina—is to heat it. Because this can be a stinky, smoky process, I like to do it outdoors, either over a gas or charcoal grill or a camp stove. The goal is to heat the wok completely, both on the bottom and the sides, to burn off the grease. That means you'll need to move the wok over the flames (if your wok has a wooden handle, protect it from the heat) to heat it from all angles. If seasoning your wok outdoors isn't an option, you can heat it on the stove top with the exhaust fan on high and the windows open.

Once you've burned off that initial layer of grease, it's time to season the pan. The best way to do this is to cook ingredients in it. But because the pan will still have some residual metal dust and grease, choose inexpensive ingredients that you don't plan to eat, such as bits of chicken or pork fat, Chinese chives, scallions, or ginger slices.

With the exhaust fan on and the windows open, heat your wok over high heat until a drop or two of water sprinkled on the hot surface evaporates on contact. Add a few tablespoons vegetable oil and heat until the oil is shimmering and smoking. Add the meat fat and other "trash" and stir-fry over high heat for 10 minutes, using the spatula or a wooden spoon to push the ingredients around the bottom and up the sides of the pan. If a fire erupts in your wok while seasoning it, turn off the heat and let it cool down. Discard these ingredients, let the wok cool down, and wash with cold water (no soap). Dry over low heat for 1 to 2 minutes. Repeat this process two more times. Your wok is now ready to use. To maintain a well-seasoned wok (and to develop the wok's nonstick patina), use it frequently.

Stir-Frying

Broccoli with Beech Mushrooms and Roasted Chile Paste

—

This is an incredibly flavorful, really simple way to prepare heartier vegetables. It's good with broccoli, but you can also substitute blanched green beans or cauliflower.

- 3 cups broccoli florets
- 2 tablespoons canola oil
- 1 teaspoon minced garlic
- 1 tablespoon roasted chile paste (see page 117)
- ¼ cup beech mushrooms
- 2 tablespoons rice wine (see page 215)
- 2 tablespoons chicken stock (see page 6) or water
- 1 tablespoon fish sauce (see page 36)

Serves 4 as part of multicourse meal

1.
Bring a medium pot of water to a boil over high heat. Add the broccoli florets and cook until crisp-tender, about 4 minutes. Drain, rinse with cold water until cool, and set aside.

2.
Heat a wok over high heat until very hot; the metal will have a matte appearance and a drop or two of water flicked onto its surface should evaporate on contact. Add the oil, garlic, chile paste, and mushrooms; toss well to coat and let cook stirring, 30 seconds.

3.
Add the broccoli and toss well, then add the rice wine, chicken stock, and fish sauce and cook, stirring, until the liquid has reduced by half, about 3 minutes. Remove from heat, transfer to a bowl and serve immediately.

Bok Choy with Baby Shiitake Mushrooms

—

Bok choy and shiitake mushrooms, flavored with rice wine, fish sauce, and garlic, is a pretty common stir-fry combination, but this recipe works just as well with an equal amount of snow or snap peas or thinly sliced summer squash. It's also especially good with Brussels sprouts, provided you have the patience to separate every leaf. Rinse the bok choy in water before you stir-fry it; the little bit of moisture that clings to the vegetable helps it steam-cook as you stir-fry.

- 3 tablespoons canola oil
- 1 teaspoon minced garlic
- ¼ pound fresh baby shiitake mushrooms, stems removed, or ¼ pound fresh regular-size shiitake mushrooms, stemmed, caps thinly sliced
- 2 pounds bok choy, rinsed and cut into 3-inch lengths
- 2 tablespoons rice wine (see page 215)
- 1½ tablespoons fish sauce (see page 36)
- 1 tablespoon chicken stock (see page 6) or water

Serves 2 to 4 as part of a multicourse meal

1.
Heat a wok over high heat until very hot; the metal will have a matte appearance and a drop or two of water flicked onto its surface should evaporate on contact. Add the oil and heat until the oil is shimmering but not smoking.

2.
Add the garlic, cook 5 seconds then add the shiitakes and stir-fry 30 seconds, until just softened. Add the bok choy and rice wine and mix together with the mushrooms and garlic.

3.
Add the fish sauce and chicken stock and cook until the bok choy is just tender, about 1 to 2 minutes, stirring frequently. If after 2 minutes the bok choy is still crunchy, cover the wok with a lid and let cook until tender.

4.
Remove from the heat, transfer to a bowl, and serve immediately.

Spinach with Caramelized Shallots

—

This is a quick, simple recipe. At the restaurant, I like to pair sweet-savory fried shallots with tender spinach, but you can substitute an equal amount of Swiss chard, kale, or tender young pea or fava shoots in place of the spinach. This recipe calls for canola oil, but you can vary the flavor of the greens by sautéing them in olive oil or chicken, pork, or beef fat.

- 3 tablespoons canola oil
- 2 tablespoons fried shallots (see page 9)
- 1 teaspoon minced garlic
- 2 pounds baby spinach, rinsed
- 2 tablespoons rice wine (see page 215)
- 1 tablespoon fish sauce (see page 36)
- 2 tablespoons chicken stock (see page 6) or water

Serves 2 to 4 as part of a multicourse meal

1.
Heat a wok over high heat until very hot; the metal will have a matte appearance and a drop or two of water flicked onto its surface should evaporate on contact. Add the oil and heat until the oil is shimmering but not smoking.

2.
Add the fried shallots and garlic, cook 10 seconds, then add the spinach and rice wine and toss well to combine. Add the fish sauce and chicken stock and continue stir-frying, tossing the ingredients together, until the spinach is just wilted, 30 seconds to 1 minute. Remove from heat, transfer to a bowl, and serve immediately.

Gulf Shrimp and Sing Qua Stir-Fry

—

Sing qua is the Cantonese name for a variety of squash with a ridged exterior and a mild flavor similar to zucchini. Also known as Chinese okra, angled luffa, or silk gourd, it can grow up to nine feet long, though the large ones can be bitter. Look for squashes twelve to eighteen inches long at Asian markets. Coating the shrimp in a little cornstarch gives them a silky texture and helps to lightly thicken the sauce. Quickly blanching the shrimp in hot oil—just enough to partially cook them, but not so much that they begin to brown—ensures they won't overcook when combined with the other ingredients.

This is a simple recipe that gives the main ingredients top billing at the table. It's also a study in contrasting textures: done correctly, the shrimp should be snappy and the *sing qua* silky. Serve this dish with steamed rice to soak up the flavorful juices.

- 1 pound sing qua (Chinese okra), peeled and sliced into ½-inch-thick slices on the diagonal (about 4 cups)
- 12 ounces medium-size shrimp, preferably from the Louisiana Gulf, peeled and halved lengthwise
- ½ cup plus 1 tablespoon canola oil
- 2 teaspoons fish sauce (see page 36)
- 1 teaspoon cornstarch
- ⅛ teaspoon freshly ground black pepper
- 10 strands finely julienned fresh ginger
- 1 teaspoon minced garlic
- 1½ tablespoons rice wine (see page 215)
- ⅛ teaspoon kosher salt

Serves 3 as part of a multicourse meal

1.
Bring a saucepan filled with water to a boil over high heat. Add the sing qua and blanch for 1 minute. Drain and set aside.

2.
In a bowl, combine the shrimp, 1 tablespoon of the oil, 1 teaspoon of the fish sauce, the cornstarch, and the pepper and mix to combine. Let stand for 10 minutes.

3.
Heat a wok over high heat until very hot; the metal will have a matte appearance and a drop or two of water flicked onto its surface should evaporate on contact. Add the remaining ½ cup oil and heat until the oil is shimmering but not smoking Add the shrimp and cook, stirring, for 30 to 45 seconds, until they begin to curl and are bright pink. Using a spider or a slotted spoon, transfer the shrimp to a bowl and set aside.

4.
Pour off all but 2 tablespoons of the oil from the wok. Return the wok to high heat. When the oil is shimmering, add the ginger and garlic and cook, stirring constantly, for 5 seconds. Return the shrimp to the wok, add the sing qua, and stir to mix. Add the wine and deglaze the pan, stirring to dislodge any browned bits. Cook, for about 3 minutes longer, until the shrimp and sing qua are cooked through.

5.
Add the remaining 1 teaspoon fish sauce and the salt, toss to mix, and transfer to a platter. Serve immediately.

Squid with Tomato and Pickled Mustard Greens

—

Seafood and tomato is a classic pairing in many countries, but pickled mustard greens takes the combination to another level (see Braised Branzino with Tomatoes and Pickled Mustard Greens on page 118 for another example). Here, the squid is quickly oil-blanched so it remains tender, then the tomato mixture is cooked down until it has thickened, at which point the squid is stirred back in. The entire dish takes about 10 minutes from start to finish.

- ½ cup canola oil
- 1 pound cleaned squid, both bodies and tentacles, with bodies halved lengthwise, then crosswise into thirds
- 1 teaspoon minced garlic
- 2 jalapeño chiles, stemmed, seeded, and julienned
- 2 cups coarsely chopped tomatoes
- ¼ cup chicken stock (see page 6) or water
- 1 tablespoon rice wine (see page 215)
- 2 teaspoons fish sauce (see page 36), plus more as needed
- ½ cup loosely packed chopped pickled mustard greens, homemade (see page 119) or store-bought, rinsed
- 1 cup scallion cut into 1½-inch-long batons

Serves 3 as part of a multicourse meal

1.
Heat a wok over high heat until hot; the metal will have a matte appearance and a drop or two of water flicked onto its surface should evaporate on contact. Add the oil and heat until shimmering but not smoking; it should register 350°F on a deep-frying thermometer. Add half of the squid and cook, stirring constantly, for 30 seconds. Using a spider or a slotted spoon, transfer the squid to a plate. Let the oil return to temperature, then cook the remaining squid the same way and add it to the plate.

2.
Pour off all but 2 tablespoons of the oil from the wok. Return the wok to high heat. When the oil is shimmering, add the garlic and chiles and cook, stirring constantly for 5 seconds. Add the tomatoes, stock, wine, and fish sauce and cook, stirring occasionally, for about 5 minutes, until the tomatoes have begun to break down and the sauce has started to thicken.

3.
Stir in the mustard greens and continue cooking, stirring occasionally, for 5 minutes longer. Stir in the squid and scallions and cook for 2 minutes more, until the scallions are just softened.

4.
Taste and adjust the seasoning with fish sauce. Transfer to a platter and serve immediately.

Black Bass with Yellow Chives and Bean Sprouts

—

This stir-fry is all about texture: silky pieces of fish contrasting with the crunch of bean sprouts and chives. For that reason, it's important not to overcook the bean sprouts. Every wok and every stove is different, so taste as you go, removing the stir-fry from the heat when the chives still have body and the sprouts still have some crunch.

The small amount of cornstarch added to the fish helps keep the delicate slices from breaking apart. Even so, be gentle: too much aggressive stirring and the slices will crumble into something resembling canned tuna.

Yellow chives, a member of the lily family, are a specialty item that can be found at Asian groceries during the spring and summer. They are grown in the dark, like white asparagus, which keeps them pale yellow, and the flavor is like a mild version of green chives. If you can't get black bass, branzino is a fine substitute.

- 2 (8-ounce) skinless black bass fillets
- 8 tablespoons plus 1 teaspoon canola oil
- 2 teaspoons cornstarch
- 1¼ teaspoons fish sauce (see page 36)
- ⅛ teaspoon kosher salt, plus more as needed
- ⅛ teaspoon freshly ground black pepper
- ½ teaspoon minced garlic
- 1½ cups yellow chives cut into 3-inch-long pieces
- 1 tablespoon rice wine (see page 215)
- 2 cups mung bean sprouts (see page 207)
- ½ cup chicken stock (see page 6)
- 10 strands finely julienned fresh ginger

Serves 3 as part of a multicourse meal

1.
Cut the fish into ½-inch-thick slices. In a small bowl, combine the fish, 1 teaspoon of the oil, ½ teaspoon of the cornstarch, ¼ teaspoon of the fish sauce, and the salt and pepper. Mix gently to combine and let stand for 10 minutes.

2.
Heat a wok over high heat until very hot; the metal will have a matte appearance and a drop or two of water flicked onto its surface should evaporate on contact. Add 2 tablespoons of the oil and heat until oil is shimmering but not smoking. Add the garlic and yellow chives and cook, stirring for 10 seconds. Add the wine and deglaze the pan, stirring to dislodge any browned bits.

3.
Add bean sprouts and ¼ cup of the stock and cook, stirring occasionally, for about 3 minutes, until the stock has reduced by half. Season with the remaining 1 teaspoon fish sauce and transfer to a warmed platter.

4.
In a small bowl, stir together the remaining 1½ teaspoons cornstarch with 1½ teaspoons warm water until smooth. Set aside.

5.
Rinse out the wok and return to high heat. When the wok is hot, add the remaining 6 tablespoons oil and heat until shimmering but not smoking. Add the fish and stir-fry gently for about 1 minute, just until cooked through.

6.
Pour off all but 1 tablespoon of the oil from the wok (leave the fish in the wok) and return the wok to high heat. When the oil is shimmering, add the ginger and cook, stirring, for 10 seconds. Add the remaining ¼ cup stock and the cornstarch slurry and mix gently to combine. Let cook for 20 seconds more, until sauce thickens slightly.

7.
Taste and adjust the seasoning with salt. Arrange the fish on top of the bean sprout-chive mixture and serve immediately.

Scrambled Eggs and Pork

—

This is one of those three-ingredient recipes that looks simple but is easy to mess up. Getting the elements right—the pork crispy, the eggs fluffy and just set—is what makes this dish great. One of the keys to success is to hand-chop the pork. Think of it as justification for buying that cleaver you've always wanted. The coarse texture allows you to crisp the meat without overcooking it; the little bit of cornstarch aids the browning.

Savory egg preparations are found throughout Asia, probably because eggs are a quick-cooking, inexpensive protein and chickens are easy to raise in a small yard. In Vietnam, these scrambled eggs are not eaten for breakfast, but for dinner, accompanied with steamed rice, a stir-fried vegetable, and maybe a whole fish. It is a true family meal, one that you'd never be served in a restaurant.

- 6 ounces boneless pork shoulder, coarsely hand-chopped (see page 52)
- 2 teaspoons fish sauce (see page 36)
- 1 teaspoon cornstarch
- ¼ teaspoon kosher salt
- ⅛ teaspoon freshly ground black pepper
- ⅓ cup canola oil
- 4 eggs

Serves 3 as part of a multicourse meal

1.
In a bowl, combine the pork, 1 teaspoon of the fish sauce, the cornstarch, and the salt and pepper. Stir to mix well and let stand for 15 minutes.

2.
Heat a wok over high heat until hot; the metal will have a matte appearance and a drop or two of water flicked onto its surface should evaporate on contact. Add the oil and heat until shimmering but not smoking. Add the pork and cook, stirring occasionally, for 5 to 7 minutes, until the meat is very well browned.

3.
While the pork is cooking, whisk together the eggs and the remaining 1 teaspoon fish sauce until well combined.

4.
Pour off all but 1 tablespoon of the oil from the wok (leave the pork in the wok) and return the wok to high heat. When the oil is shimmering, add the eggs; they should puff immediately around the edges and begin to brown. As the eggs cook, run a heatproof spatula though the center to break them up and allow them to cook more evenly, but resist the urge to constantly stir, which breaks them up too much.

5.
When the eggs are just set but still very soft, remove the wok from the heat and transfer the eggs and pork to a warmed platter. Serve immediately.

Water Spinach with Shrimp Paste

—

Water spinach, which is also known as morning glory and, in Cantonese, as *ong choy*, is actually not botanically related to spinach, despite its Western name. Nevertheless, it's a nutritious, mild green worth sampling. The stalks of water spinach are hollow and the leaves are long and tapered. Look for bunches that are deep green and not wilted. The robust condiment of shrimp paste and lime is a traditional pairing with water spinach.

- 1 tablespoon fish sauce (see page 36)
- 2 teaspoons shrimp paste (see page 215)
- 1 teaspoon freshly squeezed lime juice
- 1 teaspoon sugar
- 1 Thai chile, stemmed and minced
- 2 tablespoons canola oil
- 1 teaspoon minced garlic
- 10 strands finely julienned fresh ginger
- 1 jalapeño chile, stemmed and thinly sliced into rings
- 1 large bunch water spinach (about 2 pounds), stems trimmed and cut into 3-inch lengths
- 2 tablespoons rice wine (see page 215)

Serves 4 as part of a multicourse meal

1.
In a small bowl, combine the fish sauce, shrimp paste, lime juice, sugar, and Thai chile and stir until the sugar has dissolved. Set aside.

2.
Heat a wok over high heat until very hot; the metal will have a matte appearance and a drop or two of water flicked onto its surface should evaporate on contact. Add the oil and heat until the oil is shimmering but not smoking. Add the garlic, ginger, and jalapeño chile and cook, stirring, for 5 seconds.

3.
Add the water spinach and wine and cook, turning the greens over with tongs as they wilt (they will shrink considerably in the pan). Add the fish sauce mixture and continue cooking for 1 to 2 minutes, until all of the spinach is wilted and tender.

4.
Transfer the greens to a serving platter, leaving the excess liquid behind in the pan. Serve immediately.

Lemongrass Chicken

—

Lemongrass is used in a lot of Vietnamese cooking, but this recipe is one of the most popular dishes that calls for it. In Vietnam, lemongrass is used in two different ways. It is used as an aromatic, cut into large pieces and smashed for simmering in soups, curries, and stews, like bay leaves. It is also chopped so finely that it looks like granulated sugar and then added to dishes where it contributes an incredible fragrance and a pleasant texture that cannot be achieved by throwing the stalks into a food processor. Chopping lemongrass by hand to the proper consistency takes time, but if you're patient, you'll end up with a beautiful finished product.

- 2 tablespoons fish sauce (see page 36)
- 2 tablespoons chicken stock (see page 6) or water
- Pinch of sugar
- ¼ cup canola oil
- 1 pound skinless, boneless chicken, a mix of breast and thigh meat, cut into 1-inch cubes
- 1 cup thinly sliced red onion
- 2 teaspoons finely chopped garlic
- ¼ cup finely minced lemongrass (see page 207)
- 1 red or green jalapeño chile, stemmed and thinly sliced on the diagonal into rings
- 2 tablespoons rice wine (see page 215)
- 1 tablespoon roasted chile paste (see page 117)
- 2 scallions, trimmed and cut into 1-inch pieces
- 1 tablespoon finely chopped roasted peanuts, for garnish

Serves 3 or 4 as a part of a multicourse meal

1.
In a small bowl, whisk together fish sauce, stock, and sugar until the sugar has dissolved. Set aside.

2.
Heat a wok over high heat until hot; the metal will have a matte appearance and a drop or two of water flicked onto its surface should evaporate on contact. Add the oil and heat until shimmering but not smoking. Add the chicken and cook, turning occasionally, for 3 to 4 minutes, until lightly browned on both sides.

3.
Pour off all but 3 tablespoons of the oil from the wok (leave the chicken in the wok) and return the pan to medium-high heat. Add the onion and cook, stirring occasionally, for about 2 minutes, just until softened. Add the garlic, lemongrass, and jalapeño chile and cook for 30 seconds longer. Add the wine and deglaze the pan, stirring to dislodge any browned bits.

4.
Add the fish sauce mixture, chile paste, and scallions to the pan and continue cooking for 1 minute more, until the scallions have softened slightly and the chicken is cooked through.

5.
Transfer to a serving dish and garnish with the peanuts. Serve immediately.

Bo Luc Lac: Shaking Beef

—

This dish has been on the menu at the Slanted Door since it opened in 1995. Although I was born in Vietnam, I grew up in Northern California just as the farmers' market revolution was beginning, around the time that the legendary Berkeley restaurant Chez Panisse was really hitting its stride.

When I began to think about opening a restaurant, I knew that I wanted to serve Vietnamese food but made with the same great ingredients that the other top restaurants were using. Although I had eaten shaking beef in Vietnam, the versions that I had tried were usually made with tough beef cuts that were overcooked. But the flavors—caramelized cubes of beef and a dipping sauce of salt, pepper, and fresh lime juice—were so good that I knew it would be exceptional if I made it with better ingredients.

I started making the dish with cubes of filet mignon and cooked them to a rosy medium-rare. Later, I began using exclusively grass-fed beef, which we now get from Estancia, a US-based company that raises its beef on ranches in the States, Uruguay, and Argentina, the only place we can source the quantity we need. We use about eight hundred pounds of beef each week at The Slanted Door.

- 1½ pounds filet mignon, trimmed of excess fat and cut into 1-inch cubes
- 1 tablespoon plus 1 teaspoon sugar
- 1 teaspoon kosher salt
- 1 teaspoon freshly ground black pepper
- ½ cup plus 1 tablespoon canola oil
- ¼ cup rice vinegar
- ¼ cup mirin
- ¼ cup light soy sauce (see page 215)
- 1 tablespoon dark soy sauce (see page 215)
- 2 teaspoons fish sauce (see page 36)
- 1 cup thinly sliced red onion
- 3 whole scallions, trimmed and cut into 1-inch lengths
- 1 tablespoon finely chopped garlic
- 2 tablespoons unsalted butter
- 1 bunch watercress, tough stems removed

Dipping Sauce
- 2 teaspoons kosher salt
- 1 teaspoon freshly ground black pepper
- 4 tablespoons freshly squeezed lime juice

Serves 3 or 4 as part of a multicourse meal

1.
To marinate the beef, in a bowl, combine the beef, 1 teaspoon of the sugar, salt, pepper, and 1 tablespoon of the oil and stir to mix well. Let marinate at room temperature for 2 hours.

2.
In a bowl, whisk together the vinegar, the remaining tablespoon sugar, mirin, light and dark soy sauces, and fish sauce until the sugar has dissolved. Set aside.

3.
Divide the meat into 2 equal portions. Heat a wok over high heat until hot; the metal will have a matte appearance and a drop or two of water flicked onto its surface should evaporate on contact. Add ¼ cup of oil and heat until shimmering but not smoking. Add half of the beef in a single layer and sear for about 5 minutes, until a brown crust forms on the first side. Flip the cubes and cook for 1 minute on the second side.

4.
Add half each of the red onion and scallions and cook, stirring, about 30 seconds. Add half of the soy sauce mixture and shake the pan to coat the cubes of beef. Add half each of the garlic and butter and shake the pan to distribute evenly. Transfer to a dish and keep warm.

5.
Wipe the wok clean and return to high heat. Repeat steps 3 and 4 with the remaining ¼ cup of the oil, beef, red onion, scallions, garlic, and butter.

6.
Arrange the watercress on a platter and top with the beef. To make the dipping sauce, in a small bowl, stir together the salt and pepper and squeeze in the lime juice. Place alongside the platter for dipping the beef cubes as you eat.

Beef Bavette with Tomatoes and Thick-Cut Potatoes

—

When I first introduced this dish at my restaurant, one of my staff thought I had copied from Limón, a Peruvian restaurant in San Francisco where my friend Martin Castillo is the chef. I did not know Martin had the same dish on his menu, but *lomo saltado*, as it's called in Peru, is a classic in Peru. Steak with French fries is very popular in Vietnam, but in a departure from French tradition the two are combined this way, in a stir-fry. The only difference between the Peruvian version and the Vietnamese one is that our version has fish sauce and fresh green chiles. I make it with what is known as beef bavette, another name for skirt steak. You must have good, ripe tomatoes. The fries, which are added at the end, absorb the delicious pan juices.

- 1 pound beef bavette, skirt, or flank steak
- 2 teaspoons cornstarch
- ½ teaspoon freshly ground black pepper
- 4 tablespoons plus 1 teaspoon canola oil, plus more for deep-frying
- 1 large russet potato, peeled and cut lengthwise into batons about ⊠ inch thick
- 1 jalapeño chile, stemmed and thinly sliced into rings
- 2 teaspoons finely chopped garlic
- 4 tablespoons rice wine (see page 215)
- 4 tomatoes (such as Early Girl or Roma), cored and cut into ¾-inch wedges (about 2 cups)
- 4 tablespoons fish sauce (see page 36)
- 2 teaspoons oyster sauce (see page 214)
- 1 cup ¾-inch-long scallion batons, white and light green parts only

Serves 4 as a main course; serves 6 as part of a multicourse meal

1.
Cut the beef lengthwise with the grain into long strips about 1½ inches thick. Cut each strip across the grain on the diagonal into ¼-inch-thick slices. Transfer to a bowl and add the cornstarch, pepper and 1 teaspoon of the oil and toss to coat. Let stand at room temperature for at least 30 minutes or up to 2 hours.

2.
To cook the French fries, pour oil to a depth of 2 inches into a wok or wide, heavy-bottomed saucepan and heat to 350°F on a deep-frying thermometer. Add the potato batons and fry for 5 to 6 minutes, until deep golden brown and tender. Using a spider or a slotted spoon, transfer the batons to paper towels to drain. Set aside. Pour off the oil and reserve for another use.

3.
Divide the beef into 2 equal portions. Heat the wok over high heat until hot; the metal will have a matte appearance and a drop or two of water flicked onto its surface should evaporate on contact. Add 2 tablespoons of the oil and heat until shimmering but not smoking. Add half of the beef pieces in a single layer and cook for about 1 minute, until browned on the first side. Flip the pieces and and cook for about 1 minute more, until browned on the second side.

4.
Pour off all but 1 tablespoon of the oil from the wok (leave the beef in the wok) and return the pan to high heat. When the oil is shimmering, add half of the jalapeño slices and 1 teaspoon of the garlic and cook, stirring, for 10 seconds. Add 2 tablespoons of the wine and cook for about 30 seconds, until the wine has evaporated.

5.
Add half of the tomatoes, 2 tablespoons of the fish sauce, and 1 teaspoon of the oyster sauce and toss to combine. Cook, stirring, for 2 minutes. Stir in half of the scallions and half of the French fries and cook for 1 minute more.

6.
Transfer to a warmed serving platter. Wipe out the wok and repeat steps 3, 4, and 5 with the remaining ingredients, then add to the platter. Serve immediately.

Fried Rice
—

Fried rice is never something I intend to make, but it's something I'll cook for myself when I'm home, my wife and kids are away, and there's not a whole lot in the refrigerator. Fried rice is best made with day-old rice, so it's essentially glorified leftovers.

Scrambling the egg in the wok or sauté pan first helps prevent the rice from sticking to the pan. And while every Chinese restaurant in America seems to add frozen peas and carrot chunks to fried rice with abandon, I like to use real vegetables: shredded leafy greens, tiny steamed broccoli florets, or inch-long pieces of green bean. You can add a little shrimp or some leftover roast pork. In other words, this recipe can be made with almost anything. The only essential ingredients are rice, egg, and scallion.

This is best eaten out of a bowl, beer in hand, after a long day.

- ½ cup canola oil
- 6 ounces shrimp, peeled, deveined, and cut into small pieces
- 4 cups cooked long-grain white rice, at room temperature
- ½ teaspoon kosher salt
- ½ teaspoon sugar
- ¼ teaspoon freshly ground black pepper
- 2 eggs
- 3 cups finely shredded leafy greens (such as bok choy, Swiss chard, or spinach)
- 2 teaspoons Golden Mountain seasoning sauce (see page 214) or light soy sauce (see page 215), plus more to taste
- 2 teaspoons fish sauce (see page 36)
- ¼ cup sliced scallions, white and light green parts only

Serves 3 or 4 hungry, tired people

1.
Heat a wok over high heat; the metal will have a matte appearance and a drop or two of water flicked onto its surface should evaporate on contact. Add the oil and heat until shimmering but not smoking. Add the shrimp and cook for 1 minute, until pink. Using a spider or a slotted spoon, transfer to a small bowl and and set aside. Pour off all but 3 tablespoons of the oil from the pan into a small heatproof bowl and set the bowl aside.

2.
In a bowl, stir together the rice, salt, sugar, and black pepper, breaking up any clumps and mixing well to combine.

3.
Return the wok to high heat and heat the oil until it is shimmering. Crack the eggs into the pan. With the back of a spoon or spatula, immediately scramble the egg, smearing and spreading it around to coat as much of the bottom of the wok as possible. When the egg is no longer wet but has not yet begun to brown, add the rice and toss to combine. Continue stir-frying until the rice is heated through, about 3 minutes.

4.
Add the greens and cook, stirring, just until wilted. Add the cooked shrimp and toss to mix well. Add the seasoning sauce and fish sauce and mix well. Season to taste with additional soy and fish sauce. Remove from the heat and stir in the scallions. Transfer to a warmed platter and serve immediately.

Wok-Fried Rice Noodles with Beef and Bok Choy

—

This recipe is similar to *chow fun*, a Cantonese dish of wide rice noodles stir-fried with beef. And though it's most commonly associated with Chinese restaurants, it's also a classic Vietnamese stir-fried noodle dish. If you can find fresh wide rice noodles, this is the place to use them. Otherwise, dried noodles will work just fine.

- 10 ounces dried or 16 ounces fresh flat rice noodles, wide width (about ½-inch) (see page 12)
- 6 ounces beef flank steak, cut into 3 by ½ by ¼-inch strips
- 3 tablespoons plus 1 teaspoon canola oil, plus more for tossing with noodles
- 3 teaspoons fish sauce (see page 36)
- 3 teaspoons light soy sauce (see page 215)
- ½ teaspoon cornstarch
- ¼ teaspoon salt
- 2 cups bite-size pieces bok choy
- 1 cup fresh mung bean sprouts (see page 207)

Serves 4 as a main dish; serves 6 as part of a multicourse meal

1.
If using dried noodles, bring a large pot of water to a boil. When the water is boiling, add the noodles and cook until just barely tender (the noodles will finish cooking in the wok, so you do not want to overcook them here). Drain, rinse with cold water, and transfer to a rimmed baking sheet. Toss with a small amount of oil and let stand 15 minutes to dry slightly. If using fresh noodles, they do not need to be boiled; they can be stir-fried directly from the package.

2.
In a medium bowl, combine the beef with 1 teaspoon oil, 1 teaspoon fish sauce, 1 teaspoon soy sauce, the cornstarch, and the salt and mix well to coat. Let stand 10 minutes.

3.
Heat a wok over high heat; the metal will have a matte appearance and a drop or two of water flicked onto its surface should evaporate on contact. Add 1 tablespoon of the remaining oil and heat until shimmering but not smoking. Add the beef and stir-fry, tossing the meat in the pan, until lightly browned but still pink inside, 5 minutes. Transfer the meat to a plate, rinse the wok with water and return to high heat.

4.
Using your fingers, separate the noodles if they are sticking together. Add remaining 2 tablespoons oil to the hot wok. When hot, add the noodles and bok choy. Stir-fry 30 seconds, tossing the noodles in the wok so that they don't stick. Add the bean sprouts and remaining fish and soy sauces and cook 30 seconds longer, tossing to incorporate the ingredients. Return the cooked beef to the wok and toss with the noodles until everything is heated through and well incorporated.

5.
Transfer to a warmed serving platter and serve.

Crispy Egg Noodles with Seafood

—

The first time I had this dish was when I was about ten years old, from a stand that set up behind my family's shop in Vietnam.

What makes this dish so good is the contrasting textures. The fried noodles are crunchy, and when you add the vegetables, seafood, and gravy, they get soft and chewy in places, soaking up the sauce.

I've made a seafood version here, but you could substitute chicken, if you prefer, and vary the vegetables depending on what you have in your fridge. It's best to use homemade chicken stock, which will give you the most flavorful gravy.

- 1½ cups small broccoli florets
- ¼ cup canola oil, plus more for frying
- 1½ pounds fresh chow mein egg noodles, divided into 6 portions
- 6 tablespoons cornstarch
- 1 cup thinly sliced red onion
- ½ cup julienned carrots
- 1 cup sliced fresh shiitake mushrooms
- 12 medium-size shrimp, preferably from the Louisiana Gulf, peeled and deveined
- ½ pound cleaned squid, bodies cut into ½-inch rings
- 6 small scallops, sliced in half horizontally
- ¼ cup rice wine (see page 215)
- 5 cups chicken stock (see page 6)
- 2 tablespoons sugar
- 3 tablespoons fish sauce (see page 36)
- ¼ cup vegetarian stir-fry sauce (see page 215)
- 2 teaspoons toasted sesame oil

Serves 6

1.
Preheat the oven to 250°F. Bring a medium pot of water to a boil over high heat. When the water is boiling, add the broccoli and cook until just tender, about 5 minutes. Drain, rinse with cold water, and set aside.

2.
In a wok or heavy bottomed pot, heat 2 inches of oil to 350°F. Divide the noodles into 6 portions, and form each portion into a loose ball about 5 inches in diameter. When the oil is hot, place one ball of noodles on a spider or two slotted spoons and gently lower into the hot oil. The noodles will spread into a disc about 8 inches wide.

3.
Cook the noodles for 1 minute or until golden brown. With the spider or slotted spoons, remove the noodles from the oil and drain on paper towels. Repeat with each portion of noodles, allowing oil to return to 350°F between batches. When all of the noodles have been fried, put on a sheet pan and place in the oven to keep warm. If you fried the noodles in your wok, let the oil cool slightly, then carefully pour out into a heatproof bowl. Save for future frying or discard once it has cooled.

4.
In a small bowl, mix cornstarch with ¾ cup cold water, stirring until smooth. Set aside. Heat a wok over high heat; the metal will have a matte appearance and a drop or two of water flicked onto its surface should evaporate on contact. Add 2 tablespoons of the oil and the onions and cook, tossing frequently, until they begin to soften, about 3 minutes. Add half of the broccoli, carrots and shiitake mushrooms, toss, and cook 1 to 2 minutes more. Add half of the shrimp, squid, and scallops and cook 1 minute more, tossing frequently. Deglaze the wok with half of the rice wine and cook 30 seconds more. Add half of the chicken stock, sugar, fish sauce, stir-fry sauce, sesame oil, and cornstarch slurry. Bring to a boil, then reduce the heat so the liquid is simmering and simmer 2 minutes, until the sauce thickens slightly.

5.
Place 3 of the fried noodle disks on individual plates and divide the seafood mixture and sauce evenly over the top of the noodles.

6.
Wipe the wok clean and repeat steps 4 and 5 using the remaining ingredients. Serve immediately.

Mix-and-Match Wok-Fried Noodles

—

The best thing about stir-fried noodle dishes is that there are no rules for what they can contain. This recipe is an example of that. The basic noodle stir-frying technique works with either round rice vermicelli or flat thin rice noodles, and you can add chicken or pork, or even beef or shrimp. The vegetables, too, can vary depending on what you have in your fridge. The important thing here is to cut everything into bite-size pieces so that it cooks quickly and is easy to eat with chopsticks.

Scrambling an egg in the wok—and really smearing it around to coat the pan—helps prevent the noodles from sticking without adding lots of extra oil. Cook the egg fully before adding the noodles, however, or the egg will cling to the noodle strands, making them soggy.

- 16 ounces rice vermicelli or dried flat rice noodles, thin width (about ⅛-inch) (see page 12)
- 3 tablespoons plus 1 to 2 teaspoons canola oil
- 8 ounces chicken breast or boneless pork shoulder, cut into 3 by ½ by ¼-inch slices
- 3 teaspoons fish sauce (see page 36)
- 3 teaspoons light soy sauce (see page 215)
- 1 teaspoon cornstarch
- ½ teaspoon kosher salt
- ¼ teaspoon freshly ground black pepper
- 2 large eggs, lightly beaten
- 1 cup fresh mung bean sprouts (see page 207)
- 2 ribs celery, thinly sliced on the diagonal

Serves 4 as a main course; serves 6 as part of a multicourse meal

1.
Bring a large pot of water to a boil over high heat. If using vermicelli, add them to the pot and boil until just cooked but still firm, about 3 minutes. If using dried flat rice noodles, add them to the pot and boil until just cooked but still firm, 5 to 6 minutes. Do not overcook, because the noodles will finish cooking in the wok. Drain the noodles, rinse with cold water, and spread on a rimmed baking sheet; toss with 1 teaspoon of canola oil.

2.
In a medium bowl, combine the chicken, 1 teaspoon fish sauce, 1 teaspoon soy sauce, cornstarch, salt, pepper, and 1 teaspoon canola oil. Mix well and let stand 10 minutes.

3.
Heat a wok over high heat; the metal will have a matte appearance and a drop or two of water flicked onto its surface should evaporate on contact. Add 1 tablespoon of the oil; when the oil is hot, add the chicken and stir-fry until just cooked through, 3 to 4 minutes. Transfer the meat to a plate, rinse the wok, wipe clean, and return to high heat.

4.
Heat the remaining 2 tablespoons oil in the wok. Add the beaten eggs, smearing them all over the bottom of the wok to coat (this helps prevent the noodles from sticking). When the egg is no longer wet, but has not yet begun to brown, add the noodles, bean sprouts, celery, and remaining fish and soy sauces. Stir-fry for 2 minutes, lifting and tossing the ingredients so they are well incorporated.

5.
Add the chicken and continue stir-frying, tossing the chicken with the noodles, until all ingredients are well combined. Transfer to a warm platter and serve.

In Vietnam, no one has hulking gas grills or state-of-the-art rotisseries or smokers but cooking outdoors over live fire is common. When I was growing up, our family had a cook who prepared all of our meals over an open fire: meats were grilled on a grate over the fire, clay pots containing braises were set directly on the coals. The hearth was a multipurpose cooking space.

The enticing smell of grilled meats fills  the streets of Vietnam, where charcoal braziers are set up in restaurants and on street corners, with fans (either electric or hand) keeping small fires burning hot while sending the delicious aromas into the air.

In America, grills have gotten quite sophisticated, but our understanding of the basic principles of live-fire cooking has not. I understand the convenience of cooking on a gas grill, but I believe that grilling is something that is best done over a bed of hardwood coals, which imbues the food with an irresistible smoky flavor. Isn't that the whole point of grilling?

Building a fire for cooking is no different than building a campfire, and once you learn the basic technique, it's pretty foolproof. I like to use kindling and hardwood charcoal, eliminating the need for chemical-soaked briquettes. The key to cooking over hardwood charcoal is that you have to start the fire a good thirty minutes before you plan to cook on it. This allows the larger chunks of charcoal to break down into a thick bed of coals—you want to grill over coals, not over fire.

Successful grilling is all about controlling the fire: a deep bed of coals allows you to create a mix of temperature zones, with hotter and cooler areas so you can customize the grilling depending on whether you're cooking delicate fish or a thick pork chop.

When building the fire, I often like to create a two-zone fire, banking two-thirds of the hot coals in a thick layer on one side of my grill to create a hot zone, and raking the balance of the coals to the opposite side to create a cooler zone. Then, you can use the grill grate just as you would a pan  on the stove top: adjust the heat from hot to cool just by moving the food around the grate. This isn't necessary for all grilled dishes, since some of them, like the Pork-Stuffed Squid with Spicy Tomato Sauce (page 156), benefit from direct, hot heat. But it's a great method if you're grilling meats that have a sweet marinade (like the Grilled Pork Chops with Sweet Lemongrass Marinade, page 154) or preparing something that needs to be started over high heat and then finished over cooler heat (Rice Clay Pot with Chicken and Chinese Sausage, page 166).

Just like our old family cook, I like to think of the grill as a multipurpose cooking surface. Of course, you can cook vegetables and meats directly on the grate. But if you maximize the grill surface, thinking of it in the same way you think of your stove top, you can prepare an entire meal, start to finish, outdoors. For example, as friends gather and have a cocktail, use a cast-iron frying pan on the grill grate to make Clams with Crispy Pork Belly (page 158) and grill skewers of Chicken Satay (page 162) alongside. Or, cook a Chinese-style rice clay pot (page 166) on the grate as the main event and accompany it with a Grilled Whole Fish (page 161) cooked on a cast-iron griddle placed on the grate, a technique that allows the fish to pick up some smoky flavor without any chance of it sticking to the metal bars.

Understanding the possibilities of live-fire cooking, which extend far beyond burgers, will change the way you cook.

START GRILL 30 MIN. PRIOR TO USE.

AIR VENT IS OPEN.   MUST CLEAN

CHARCOAL.

PLACE COAL ON ONE SIDE OF GRILL. NOT CENTER.

HIGH TEMP   LOW TEMP

Grilled Pork Chops with Sweet Lemongrass Marinade
—

This flavorful lemongrass marinade is pretty common in Vietnam, where it's used on thin pork chops that are quickly grilled over a hot fire. Because the marinade has a lot of sugar, grilling the meat is the only way to go. If you try to pan-fry the pork chops, the sugar will burn before the meat is cooked through.

These chops are best grilled over a two-zone fire. Start the meat on the hot side of the grill, which will sear the meat and begin to caramelize the sugar in the marinade, then move them to the cooler side to cook them through.

The combination of salty and sweet is pretty irresistible, and the hand-chopped lemongrass adds fragrance and texture. I like to serve the pork with bowls of rice or vermicelli noodles (see page 170). Use the best pork you can get, and don't trim off all of the fat. It helps baste the chops as they cook.

- ¾ cup sugar
- ¼ cup plus 1 tablespoon fish sauce (see page 36)
- 1 lemongrass stalk, finely chopped (see page 207)
- 1½ tablespoons minced garlic
- 2 tablespoons minced shallot
- 1 Thai chile, stemmed and finely chopped
- ¼ teaspoon freshly ground black pepper
- 3 bone-in center cut pork chops, each about 12 ounces and 1 inch thick

Serves 6 as a main course

1.
In a bowl, combine the sugar, fish sauce, lemongrass, garlic, shallot, chile, and black pepper and whisk until the sugar dissolves. Arrange the pork chops in a rimmed dish in a single layer. Pour the marinade over, cover with plastic wrap, and let marinate at room temperature for 1 to 2 hours. (The pork can also be refrigerated overnight. Bring meat to room temperature before grilling).

2.
Prepare a hot fire in a charcoal grill (you should be able to hold your hand 1 to 2 inches above the grate for only 2 to 3 seconds). When the coals are ready, push two-thirds of the coals to one-half of the grill, creating a hot zone; spread the remaining one-third on the opposite side of the grill to create a cooler zone.

3.
Remove the pork chops from the marinade and discard the marinade. Place the chops on the hottest part of the grill. Let cook for 1 minute, then flip and cook for 1 minute on the second side.

4.
Move the chops to the cooler side of the grill and cook, turning once, for about 10 minutes total, until an instant-read thermometer inserted into the thickest part of the chop registers 140°F, raking over coals from the hotter side of the grill if necessary to maintain an even temperature. Spritz any flare-ups with a spray bottle filled with water.

5.
Transfer the chops to a large plate, tent with aluminum foil, and let stand for 10 minutes. Cut the meat from the bone and slice the meat across the grain on the diagonal. Transfer the slices and bones to a serving platter and serve.

Pork-Stuffed Squid with Spicy Tomato Sauce
—

Squid bodies make perfect little pockets for holding fillings of all kinds. I grew up eating these plump squid, which are served all over Vietnam stuffed with many different mixtures. My favorite stuffing is this combination of cellophane noodles and pork. I always cook the filling first. Otherwise, you risk overcooking the squid while you wait for the filling to cook through.

To make stuffing the squid easier, choose larger bodies. And don't overstuff them, or they may burst on the grill. If you are lazy and you want to use jarred tomato sauce, I don't have a problem with that. But the filling is much better if you hand-chop the pork rather then buying preground meat.

Tomato Sauce
- 2 pounds ripe tomatoes (such as Roma or Early Girl), cored and diced
- 2 tablespoons canola oil
- ¾ cup thinly sliced shallots
- 2 teaspoons minced garlic
- 2 Thai chiles, stemmed and minced
- ¾ cup chicken stock (see page 6)
- 2 tablespoons rice wine (see page 215)
- 1 tablespoon fish sauce (see page 36)

Squid
- 12 ounces pork shoulder, finely hand-chopped (see page 52), or ground pork
- 1½ teaspoons sugar
- 1 tablespoon plus 2 teaspoons fish sauce (see page 36)
- ½ teaspoon freshly ground black pepper, plus more for seasoning
- ¼ cup plus 2 tablespoons canola oil
- ½ cup finely diced yellow onion
- 1 teaspoon minced garlic
- ½ cup finely diced fresh shiitake mushrooms
- ½ cup dried wood ear or shiitake mushrooms (see page 210) soaked in hot water to cover for about 15 minutes until softened, drained, trimmed or stems discarded, and finely chopped
- 3 tablespoons oyster sauce (see page 214) or vegetarian stir-fry sauce (see page 215)
- 1 teaspoon toasted sesame oil
- ¼ teaspoon ground white pepper, plus more for seasoning
- 1 (2-ounce) package cellophane noodles (see page 12), soaked in very hot water to cover for 10 to 15 minutes until softened, drained, and cut into 1-inch lengths
- 1 cup thinly sliced scallions, white and light green part only
- 18 whole large squid, cleaned with tentacles separated from bodies and reserved
- Kosher salt
- ¼ cup chopped fresh basil, for garnish

Serves 6 as an appetizer

1.

To make the sauce, prepare a hot fire for direct-heat grilling in a charcoal grill (you should be able to hold your hand 1 to 2 inches above the grate for only 2 to 3 seconds). When the coals are ready, put the tomatoes directly on the grate and grill, turning as needed, until the skins are evenly blackened. Transfer to a bowl and let cool until they can be handled, then peel, discard the skins, and coarsely chop. If you are preparing the sauce and squid on the same day, maintain the bed of coals.

2.

In a saucepan, heat the oil over medium heat. Add the shallots and cook, stirring occasionally, for about 3 minutes, until light golden brown. Add the garlic and chiles and cook for 45 seconds more.

3.

Stir in the stock, wine, and tomatoes and bring to a boil. Decrease the heat so the mixture is at a gentle simmer and cook, stirring occasionally, for about 45 minutes, until the tomatoes have completely broken down and the liquid has reduced by a third. Remove from the heat, stir in the fish sauce, and keep warm. (The sauce can be made a day ahead, cooled, covered, and refrigerated; reheat before using.)

4.

In a bowl, combine the pork, sugar, 2 teaspoons of the fish sauce, and the black pepper and mix well. In a large sauté pan, heat ¼ cup of the canola oil over medium-high heat. When the oil is hot, add the pork and cook, breaking it up with a wooden spoon, for about 5 minutes, until no pink remains.

5.

Add the onion and garlic and cook, stirring, for 1 minute. Add the fresh and dried mushrooms, oyster sauce, sesame oil, the remaining 1 tablespoon fish sauce, and the white pepper and stir to combine. Stir in the cellophane noodles and scallions and remove from the heat. Spread the mixture on a rimmed baking sheet and let cool to room temperature.

6.

When the filling has cooled, transfer it to a piping bag fitted with a ½-inch plain tip or a resealable plastic bag with one corner cut off. Working with 1 squid body at a time, pipe the filling into the body, stopping within ½ inch of the opening. Seal the body closed by threading a toothpick through the open end. Repeat with the remaining squid bodies and filling. As the squid bodies are stuffed, place them in a single layer on a clean rimmed baking sheet or a platter. When all of the bodies have been stuffed, drizzle 1 tablespoon of the canola oil evenly over them, then season them with salt and pepper.

7.

If you have not been maintaining the fire, prepare the fire once again as directed in step 1. In a bowl, toss the tentacles with the remaining 1 tablespoon canola oil and season with salt and pepper. Put the stuffed squid on the grate and grill, turning once, for about 6 minutes, until lightly charred on both sides. Using tongs or a spatula, carefully remove the squid to a plate and slide the toothpick out of each squid.

8.

Place a cast-iron frying pan on the grill grate. When the pan is hot, add the tentacles and cook, stirring occasionally, for 6 to 8 minutes, until the juices begin to caramelize. Remove the pan from the grill.

9.

Pour the warm tomato sauce on a large platter and arrange the squid on top. Scatter the tentacles over the squid, sprinkle with salt and pepper, then garnish with the basil. Serve immediately.

How to Clean a Squid

Whole squid are much less expensive than cleaned squid, and cleaning them is easy. First, cut the head from the body, taking care not to cut the ink sac. Reach into the body and pull out the clear piece of cartilage and guts and discard, then pull off the purple membrane on the exterior of the body and discard. Rinse and set aside. Cut the tentacles from the head just below the eyes and ink sac and discard the eyes and sac. At the center of the tentacles is a small, hard beak; squeeze to remove and discard. The squid is now ready to cook.

Clams with Crispy Pork Belly and Thai Basil
—

Nearly every food culture has some version of surf and turf, and the combination of shellfish with cured pork is pretty common. This recipe demonstrates the versatility of the grill: the clams and pork are cooked in a cast-iron frying pan set on the grill grate, picking up a hint of smoky flavor. If you don't want to build a fire, you can cook this recipe on the stove top.

- 1 cup chicken stock (see page 6)
- 1 tablespoon fish sauce (see page 36)
- 2 teaspoons sugar
- ½ pound skin-off pork belly, sliced ⅛ inch thick, or thick-cut bacon slices
- ½ cup thinly sliced shallots
- 2 Thai chiles, stemmed and minced
- 2 small jalapeño chiles, stemmed, seeded, and julienned
- 2 by 1-inch piece fresh ginger, peeled and julienned
- 2 teaspoons minced garlic
- 2 teaspoons roasted chile paste (see page 117)
- 3 pounds Manila clams, scrubbed
- ¼ cup rice wine (see page 215)
- ½ cup fresh Thai basil leaves (see page 213)

Serves 4 to 6 as a appetizer

1.
In a measuring cup or small bowl, stir together the stock, fish sauce, and sugar until the sugar has dissolved. Set aside.

2.
Prepare a hot fire for direct-heat grilling in a charcoal grill (you should be able to hold your hand 1 to 2 inches above grate for only 2 to 3 seconds). When the coals are ready, place a deep 12-inch cast-iron frying pan on the grill grate and let preheat for 2 minutes.

3.
Add the pork belly slices in a single layer to the hot pan and cook, turning occasionally, for about 8 minutes, until some of the fat has rendered and the meat is golden brown. Pour off all but about 3 tablespoons of the accumulated fat from the pan (keep the pork in the pan) and return the pan to the grate. Add the shallots, chiles, and ginger and cook, stirring occasionally, for 1 minute. Add the garlic and chile paste and cook for 30 seconds more.

4.
Add the clams and rice wine, pour in the stock mixture, and then add the basil. Cover the pan (a metal bowl or wok lid works well) and cook, uncovering and stirring occasionally, for about 10 minutes, until all of the the clams have opened.

5.
Remove the pan from the grill and pour the clams, pork belly, and juices onto a rimmed serving dish, discarding any clams that failed to open. Serve immediately.

Grilled Whole Fish
—

The goal here is a crisp-skinned fish that is imbued with smoke from the grill and whose flesh is gently perfumed by the herbs and citrus in the cavity. Fish is notoriously tricky to grill because its skin tends to stick to the grate. To avoid this, I cook the fish on a cast-iron griddle or frying pan set on the grate. The fish still picks up some flavor from the fire, but it doesn't fall apart during cooking.

Let the pan get hot before you add the fish, and flip the fish only once, after the first side is a deep golden brown. Resist the urge to fiddle with the fish or you'll destroy the delicate flesh and crisp skin. I like branzino, but this recipe will work with any small whole fish.

- 1 (1½- to 2-pound) whole branzino, cleaned with head and tail intact
- Kosher salt and freshly ground black pepper
- 1 by 1-inch piece fresh ginger, cut into thin coins
- 2 large Thai basil sprigs (see page 213)
- 2 large cilantro sprigs
- 3 thin lemon slices
- 3 thin lime slices
- 2 tablespoons canola or olive oil

Dipping Sauce
- 2½ tablespoons freshly squeezed lime juice
- 2 tablespoons fish sauce (see page 36)
- 2 teaspoons sugar
- 1 teaspoon peeled and minced fresh ginger
- ¼ teaspoon minced garlic
- ¼ teaspoon minced Thai chile

Serves 3 as part of a multicourse meal

1.
Prepare a hot fire for direct-heat grilling in a charcoal grill (you should be able to hold you hand 1 to 2 inches above the grate for only 2 to 3 seconds). When the coals are ready, place a cast-iron griddle or large cast-iron frying pan on the grill grate and let it preheat until very hot.

2.
While the fire is reaching temperature, rinse the fish in cold water and pat dry with paper towels. Season the fish inside and out with salt and pepper, then stuff the cavity with the ginger, basil, cilantro, and lemon and lime slices. Drizzle the oil on both sides of the fish and set aside.

3.
To make the sauce, in a small bowl, stir together lime juice, fish sauce, sugar, ginger, garlic, and Thai chile until the sugar has dissolved. Set aside.

4.
When the griddle or pan is very hot, add the fish and cook it without moving it for about 6 minutes until the skin is a deep golden brown and is no longer sticking to the griddle. To check, gently try to lift the fish; if it does not release easily, continue to cook until it does.

5.
With a large, wide spatula centered at the middle of the fish, flip the fish and cook on the second side until golden brown. After 1 minute, begin checking to see if the fish is done. Insert the tip of a knife into the fish and wiggle it gently; the flesh should be barely clinging to the bone. If you feel resistance, continue cooking, repeating the test until the flesh offers no resistance.

6.
Transfer the fish to a platter and serve immediately. Accompany with the dipping sauce.

Grilling

Chicken Satay with Peanut Sauce

—

A delicious snack, satay is found everywhere on the streets of Vietnam. Unfortunately, it has become a casualty of poorly catered events in the States, where it is often served bland and cold. The best satay is flavorful and juicy and is eaten the minute it comes off the grill. Because the pieces of meat on each skewer are so small, they don't take well to precooking. Put the sticks on the grill just before you are ready to eat.

- 2½ pounds skinless, boneless chicken thighs
- ¾ cup sliced shallots
- ¾ cup shallot oil (see page 9) or canola oil
- 2 tablespoons minced garlic
- 1½ tablespoons roasted chile paste (see page 117)
- 2 tablespoons sugar
- 2 teaspoons kosher salt
- 2 teaspoons mild Madras curry powder
- Peanut sauce (see page 47)
- Sriracha sauce, for seasoning
- 20 to 25 (10-inch) bamboo skewers

Makes 20 to 25 skewers; serves 10 to 12 as an appetizer

1.
Trim any visible fat from the chicken thighs, then cut the thighs into long strips, about 1-inch wide. Put the chicken into a bowl and set aside.

2.
To make the marinade, in a food processor or blender, combine the shallots and shallot oil and process until smooth. Add the garlic, chile paste, sugar, salt, and curry powder and process until smooth.

3.
Add the marinade to the chicken and mix well to coat evenly. Cover and refrigerate for 3 hours. In a shallow dish, immerse the bamboo skewers in water to cover.

4.
Prepare a medium-hot fire for direct-heat grilling in a charcoal grill (you should be able to hold your hand 1 inch above the grate for only 3 to 4 seconds).

5.
Just before the coals are ready, drain the skewers and thread 1 strip of chicken lengthwise onto each skewer, taking care to insert the skewer through the center of each strip. Do not leave the tip of the skewer exposed or it will burn.

6.
Place the skewers on the grill grate and cook, turning once, for 2 to 3 minutes on each side, until well browned and opaque throughout.

7.
In a small bowl, stir together the peanut sauce with Sriracha to taste. Transfer the skewers to a large platter and serve immediately, accompanied with the sauce.

Grilled Five-Spice Chicken with Tamarind Sauce

—

This marinade is a bit more heavily seasoned than most Vietnamese meat marinades. It uses both fermented red bean curd, which is intensely salty, and five-spice powder (which often contains more than five spices), a popular seasoning blend for duck and other poultry recipes. The tartness of the tamarind sauce, which is made from the pulp in the pods of the tamarind tree, adds another layer of complexity.

I learned this recipe from a Vietnamese woman who worked in the kitchen at the original Slanted Door, but I don't think it originated in Vietnam. It seems like something that was created in the States, where dishes are often made to seem Asian with the addition of ingredients like five-spice powder. Origins aside, this is a crowd-pleaser. We make it with chicken breast (one of the few times I recommend using breasts), but you can use chicken thighs, if you prefer. Serve with steamed rice and a green vegetable.

- 1 cup fish sauce (see page 36)
- ½ cup light soy sauce (see page 215)
- ¼ cup minced garlic
- ¾ cup minced shallots
- 2 to 3 Thai chiles, stemmed and minced
- 1½ cubes fermented red bean curd (see page 206), mashed (about 1 tablespoon)
- 1 teaspoon five-spice powder (see page 205)
- 6 (5-ounce) skin-on, boneless chicken breasts

Sauce
- 6 ounces seedless tamarind pulp (see page 212)
- 2 tablespoons sugar
- 2 teaspoons fish sauce (see page 36)

Serves 6 as a main course

1.
In a large bowl, whisk together the fish sauce, soy sauce, garlic, shallots, chiles, bean curd, and five-spice powder. Add the chicken to the marinade and turn to coat evenly. Cover and let marinate at room temperature for up to 2 hours or in the refrigerator for up to overnight. If refrigerating, bring to room temperature before grilling.

2.
To make the sauce, in a small saucepan, combine the tamarind pulp and 1½ cups water and bring to a boil over high heat. Decrease the heat so the mixture is at a gentle simmer and simmer for about 20 minutes, until the tamarind pulp has softened completely and can easily be pressed against the side of the pan with the back of a spoon.

3.
Remove from the heat and strain through a fine-mesh sieve placed over a bowl, pressing on the solids with a rubber spatula to force through as much pulp as possible. The liquid should have the consistency of ketchup. Discard the contents of the sieve. While the liquid is still warm, add the sugar and fish sauce and stir until the sugar has dissolved. Set aside.

4.
Prepare a medium fire in a charcoal grill (you should be able to hold your hand 1 inch above the grate for only 4 to 5 seconds). When the coals are ready, push two-thirds of the coals to one-half of the grill, creating a hot zone; spread the remaining one-third on the opposite side of the grill to create a cooler zone.

5.
Arrange the chicken pieces, skin side down, on the grate over the hottest part of the grill and cook them without moving them for 6 minutes, or until well browned on the first side. Using tongs or a spatula, flip the chicken and move to the cooler side of the grill; cook for about 4 minutes more, or until browned on the second side and no longer pink at the center when tested with a knife.

6.
Transfer the chicken to a platter and serve immediately. Accompany with the tamarind sauce, inviting diners to spoon it over their own servings.

164

Spicy Mango Salad

—

I had this salad on my most recent trip to Vietnam. Look for mangoes that are firm yet ripe. You want them to have a little crunch. This salad is fiery, but once you start eating it, it's hard to stop, even as your lips start to tingle. To temper the heat, serve it alongside grilled meats, like the lemongrass pork chops on page 154.

- 1 tablespoon sugar
- 1 small clove garlic
- ½ teaspoon minced Thai chile
- ¼ teaspoon kosher salt
- ¼ cup plus 1 tablespoon freshly squeezed lime juice
- ¼ cup fish sauce (see page 36)
- 4 firm ripe mangoes
- ¼ teaspoon cayenne pepper

Serves 6 as a side dish

1.
To make the dressing, in a mortar, combine the sugar, garlic, chile, and salt and pound with a pestle until finely mashed. Transfer to a large bowl, add the lime juice and fish sauce, and stir well to combine.

2.
Stand 1 mango, stem end down, on a cutting board. Using a large, sharp knife, cut straight down along one side of the large, flat oval pit. Then cut down along the opposite side of the pit. Put one-half of the mango, skin side down, on a cutting board and, cut it lengthwise into slices about ⅛ inch thick, cutting to but not through the skin. Using a small paring knife, cut the slices away from the peel. Repeat with the remaining mango half and then with the remaining 3 mangoes.

3.
Add the mango slices to the dressing and toss to coat evenly. Sprinkle with the cayenne and serve.

Pomelo Salad

—

Native to Southeast Asia, the pomelo is a citrus fruit that resembles an overgrown grapefruit, with a thick peel and a similar flavor, though it is usually less tart. In America, pomelos are sold during the winter months. I like to make this salad late in the season, when the fruit is a little less juicy but the flavor is more concentrated. In Vietnam and China, the pomelo is a symbol of prosperity, so the fruit is often served at New Year's celebrations. Bright and fresh, it's a fine companion to rich grilled meats.

- 2½ tablespoons freshly squeezed lemon juice
- 2 tablespoons fish sauce (see page 36)
- 1 tablespoon shallot oil (see page 9) or canola oil
- 1 tablespoon sugar
- ¼ teaspoon minced Thai chile
- ¼ teaspoon kosher salt
- 4 large pomelos
- 6 cups frisée
- 1 cup thinly sliced red onion
- ¼ cup chopped fresh *rau ram* (see page 210) or spearmint
- Fried shallots (see page 9), for garnish

Serves 6 as an appetizer or side dish

1.
To make the dressing, in a small bowl, whisk together the lemon juice, fish sauce, shallot oil, sugar, chile, salt, and 1 tablespoon water until the sugar has dissolved.

2.
Working with 1 pomelo at a time and using a sharp knife, cut off both ends of the fruit so it will stand upright on your cutting board. Stand the pomelo on the board and slice downward, following the curve of the fruit, to cut away the thick peel and pith, revealing the flesh. Then, holding the fruit in your nondominant hand, cut along both sides of each segment to release it from the membrane. Cut the segments into bite-size pieces. Repeat with remaining pomelos.

3.
In a large bowl, combine the frisée, onion, *rau ram*, and pomelo pieces. Pour the dressing over the ingredients and toss to coat evenly. Garnish with the fried shallots and serve.

Rice Clay Pot with Chicken and Chinese Sausage

—

I call this Chinese paella. Made with chicken stock, chicken and Chinese sausage are added, and the flavors of each meld with the rice, enhancing what would otherwise be a pretty one-dimensional dish.

The term "Chinese sausage" is most commonly applied to a dried pork sausage formed into skinny links about six inches long. Known as *lap cheong* in Cantonese, the good ones are usually seasoned with rice wine and sugar and can be found in any Asian market. Do not substitute another type of pork sausage. It won't have the right flavor or texture.

The most challenging part of this recipe is resisting the urge to open the pot and check on the rice or, worse yet, stirring it as it cooks. Stirring the rice will disturb the absorption and you'll end up with rice that's too wet on the bottom and too dry on top. Of course, you can make this dish on a stove top, but a rice clay pot fresh from the grill is a beautiful sight.

- 2 cups long-grain jasmine rice
- 5 tablespoons rendered chicken fat or olive oil
- 4 cups chicken stock (see page 6)
- 2 skinless, boneless chicken thighs, cubed
- 6 dried shiitake mushrooms (see page 210), stems discarded, and caps halved
- 1 teaspoon minced garlic
- 1 teaspoon kosher salt
- ½ teaspoon freshly ground black pepper
- ½ teaspoon sugar
- 1 teaspoon cornstarch
- 2 Chinese sausages (see page 203), cut into ¼-inch lengths
- Light soy sauce (see page 215), for serving

Serves 4 to 6 as part of a multicourse meal

1.
Prepare a medium fire in a charcoal grill (you should be able to hold your hand 1 inch above the grate for only 4 to 5 seconds). When the coals are ready, push two-thirds of the coals to one-half of the grill, creating a hot zone; spread the remaining one-third on the opposite side of the grill to create a cooler zone.

2.
Place a large clay pot or Dutch oven on the hot side of the grill and add 2 tablespoons of the chicken fat. When the fat is hot, add the rice and toast, tossing frequently, for 4 to 5 minutes, until the rice starts to turn opaque.

3.
Add the stock and bring to a boil. Add 2 tablespoons of the chicken fat and simmer, uncovered, for 10 minutes. If the liquid is bubbling too ferociously, move the clay pot toward the cooler side of the grill.

4.
In a small bowl, combine the chicken, mushrooms, garlic, salt, pepper, sugar, cornstarch, and the remaining 1 tablespoon chicken fat and stir to mix well. Let stand for 5 minutes.

5.
Check the rice: the stock should be almost reduced by half and the rice will still be a little loose and wet. Add the chicken mixture and sausage and mix well. Move the pot to the cooler side of the grill and continue cooking, uncovered, until bubbling steam channels start to form in the rice mixture. The mixture should be bubbling gently; if necessary, push some coals from the hotter side of the grill to the cooler side.

6.
Cover and continue to cook slowly for 15 to 20 minutes, until the stock is completely absorbed. Rake more coals under the clay pot as necessary to keep the mixture bubbling gently. Do not stir, and do not open the lid.

7.
Check the rice for doneness after about 15 minutes. All of the stock should be absorbed and the rice should be fully cooked but be slightly firm at the center of each grain. Serve warm, accompanied with soy sauce.

Roasted Eggplant and Leek Salad

—

Eggplant is eaten throughout Vietnam, usually either fried or grilled. Grilling gives it a silky texture and a smoky flavor that contrasts well with the leeks, which become sweeter when cooked. This salad is good on its own, or alongside the grilled lemongrass pork chops on page 154 or any other simple grilled meat.

- 4 Rosa Bianca or globe eggplants (about 3½ pounds total)
- Kosher salt
- 12 baby leeks, white and light green parts only, halved lengthwise
- 4 tablespoons canola oil
- Freshly ground black pepper
- 1½ cups loosely packed fresh cilantro leaves, coarsely chopped
- ½ cup spicy soy sauce (see page 71)
- 1 tablespoon freshly squeezed lime juice

Serves 6 as a side dish or part of a multicourse meal

1.
Trim the stem end of each eggplant, peel and slice lengthwise into 1-inch slices. Sprinkle with salt and set aside to drain, 1 hour. After an hour, pat slices dry with a paper towel.

2.
While the eggplant slices are draining, prepare a medium fire for direct-heat grilling in a charcoal grill (you should be able to hold your hand 1 inch above the grate for only 4 to 5 seconds).

3.
When the coals are ready, drizzle the leeks with 2 tablespoons of the oil and sprinkle with salt and pepper. Place the leeks on the grate and cook, turning as needed, for about 15 minutes, until soft and charred in spots. Transfer to a plate, cover with plastic wrap, and let steam while you cook the eggplant.

4.
Drizzle the eggplant slices on both sides with the remaining 2 tablespoons oil, then sprinkle on both sides with salt and pepper. Grill the slices, turning occasionally, for about 20 minutes, until very soft and browned.

5.
Remove the eggplant slices from the grill. When cool enough to handle, cut into ½-inch cubes and transfer to a serving bowl. Cut the leeks crosswise into 1-inch-thick slices and add to the eggplant. Add the cilantro and toss to combine.

6.
In a small bowl, whisk together the spicy soy sauce and lime juice. Pour over the eggplant-leek mixture and toss to coat evenly. Season with additional salt and pepper and serve.

Vermicelli (Bun) Bowls

—

In Vietnam, bowls of cool rice vermicelli, topped with herbs, pickled carrots, and grilled meat or pieces of fried imperial rolls, are a popular lunch item. The beauty of this recipe is that it's flexible; you can make it with almost any sort of leftover grilled meat you might have (though we've suggested some options). It's especially good for a crowd, because people can customize their own bowls, and also nice in summertime, when a cool main course is especially welcome. For six people, plan on about 1 pound dried rice vermicelli or 1 batch of fresh rice noodles.

- Fresh rice noodles (see page 172) or dried rice vermicelli (see page 12), cooked, drained, and cooled
- Pickled carrots (see page 35)
- Shredded lettuce
- Spearmint springs
- Cilantro sprigs
- Chopped peanuts

One (or more) of the following:
- Lemongrass Pork (see page 55)
- Grilled Five-Spice Chicken (see page 164)
- Grilled Shrimp (see page 171)
- Imperial Rolls (see page 179)
- Flavored fish sauce, for dressing (see page 35)

1.
Put the cooked, cooled rice noodles into individual bowls, then arrange the garnishes, encouraging diners to build their own bowls, adding pickled carrots, lettuce, mint, cilantro leaves, and chopped peanuts.

2.
Top with pieces of grilled meat, shrimp, and imperial rolls, and dress with spoonfuls of flavored fish sauce.

Grilled Sweet Potatoes with Cilantro, Scallions, and Lime

—

The Vietnamese like their sugar, and sweet potatoes are a favored vegetable. The most basic preparations involve grilling sweet potatoes whole, then cutting them into pieces and dipping them in sugar (this might sound weird, but then this is the country that tops sweet potatoes with marshmallows for Thanksgiving).

This is a different take on the dish. Steaming the sweet potatoes first ensures they won't char on the grill before they're cooked through, and the lime zest adds a bright note to the candy-like vegetable.

- 3 pounds sweet potatoes, peeled, cut in half lengthwise and sliced on the bias into ½-inch thick slices
- ½ cup canola oil
- Kosher salt and freshly ground black pepper
- ½ cup scallion oil (see page 120)
- ½ cup chopped cilantro
- Zest from 3 limes

Serves 6 as a side dish

1.
Fill a large wok or stock-pot with water. Place a three-layer bamboo steamer in the wok or over the top of the pot, taking care that the water does not touch the bottom of the steamer. Bring the water to a boil.

2.
Arrange the sweet potatoes in a single layer in each layer of the bamboo steamer. Cover and steam 5 to 6 minutes, until the sweet potatoes are just tender. Transfer to a sheet pan, drizzle with oil, and sprinkle with salt and pepper.

3.
Prepare a medium-hot fire for direct-heat grilling in a charcoal grill (you should be able to hold your hand 1 inch above the grate only 3 to 4 seconds). Put the sweet potatoes on the grate and grill, turning once, about 4 to 5 minutes per side, until they are a deep golden brown.

4.
Transfer the sweet potatoes to a large mixing bowl. Add the scallion oil, cilantro, and lime zest. Toss well to coat and season with additional salt and pepper to taste.

Simple Grilled Shrimp

—

The sugar in this mixture helps the shrimp caramelize on the grill during their short cooking time. Though they are good on their own, with rice and a vegetable on the side, we typically serve them as one component of a vermicelli bowl (page 170).

- ½ cup white sugar
- 2 tablespoons kosher salt
- 1 tablespoon minced garlic
- 1½ teaspoons freshly ground black pepper
- 2 tablespoons canola oil
- 1 pound medium-size shrimp, peeled and deveined

Serves 4 as a main course

1.
In a medium bowl, combine the sugar, salt, garlic, and black pepper. Pour ¾ cup of hot water over the mixture and stir until the sugar and salt have dissolved completely. Stir in the oil and let cool to room temperature before using.

2.
Prepare a medium-hot fire for direct-heat grilling in a charcoal grill (you should be able to hold you hand 1 inch above the grate only 3 to 4 seconds). Add the shrimp to the sugar mixture and toss to coat. Transfer the shrimp to the grill and cook, turning once, 2 minutes on each side, until the shrimp are bright pink and opaque throughout.

3.
Transfer to a platter and serve, or use as component of a vermicelli bowl.

Rice Noodles

—

Dried rice noodles are readily available, but homemade fresh noodles are a fun project. If you've ever made the light pastry dough known as pâte à choux (the base for gougères and profiteroles), the first step to making the noodle dough will be familiar. The flour and water are mixed together, then cooked on the stove top until thick (this step also cooks out the raw-flour taste).

This is a two-person operation: once the paste thickens, one person will need to hold the pot down while the other stirs continuously. You will need a potato ricer for extruding the spaghetti-like noodles. The flavor of these noodles improves if you let the initial rice flour-water mixture ferment at room temperature for four days. While not essential to the success of the recipes, it does lend a nice tanginess to the finished noodles. However, if you are in a rush, you can let it soak overnight. The noodles can be used in Bún Bò Hue (page 16) or as the base for noodle bowls (page 170).

- 4 cups rice flour (see page 210), plus more for dusting
- 3½ cups water
- 3 tablespoons shallot oil (see page 9) or canola oil
- 1 cup tapioca starch (see page 212)

Makes about 3 pounds (8 to 10 cups cooked noodles)

1.
In a bowl, whisk together the rice flour and 3½ cups water until smooth. Cover and allow to ferment at room temperature for 4 days.

2.
Carefully pour out 1½ cups water from the settled rice flour. Add ¼ cup fresh water to the batter and stir until smooth.

3.
Bring a large stockpot of salted water to a boil over high heat. Keep the water hot while you prepare the dough.

4.
In a heavy-bottomed 4- to 6-quart pot, heat the oil over high heat. When the oil is hot, add the batter and turn down the heat to low. This is a two-person job: one person needs to stabilize the pot while the other one quickly and firmly stirs the batter with a wooden spoon. The dough will begin to thicken. Continue cooking, stirring continuously, for 5 to 8 minutes, until the dough is a thick, firm paste. If any dough sticks to the sides of the pot, do not scrape it off.

5.
Transfer the dough to a stand mixer fitted with the dough hook and add tapioca starch. Mix on medium speed for about 10 minutes, until it forms a sticky ball.

6.
Bring the water back to a boil, then adjust the heat to keep it at a vigorous simmer. While the water is heating, dust a clean work surface with flour, transfer the dough to it, and knead for another 5 minutes, until smooth. Cover the dough with plastic wrap to prevent it from drying out.

7.
Prepare a large ice-water bath and place it near the stove. Put 1½ cups of the dough into a potato ricer, keeping the remaining dough covered. Position the ricer directly above the center of the pot of boiling water and press firmly to extrude the noodles. As you press, smoothly lower the ricer close to the water and shake it gently from side to side to break the ends of the noodles free, allowing the noodles to fall into the simmering water. Simmer the noodles for 1½ to 2 minutes, until they bunch up to one side of the pot. With a spider or tongs, carefully transfer the noodles to the ice-water bath. Once cool, transfer to a colander and let drain. Repeat with the remaining dough, replacing the ice water as needed. When all the noodles have been cooked and cooled, rinse the noodles under cold running water to remove excess starch. Drain the noodles. The noodles are best used the same day they are made, but they can be covered and refrigerated for up to 1 day.

Nobody wants to fry at home, but everyone likes to eat fried food. There's the fear of the mess, of the smell, of the danger, of the hassle of disposing of used oil. But these are all small prices to pay for crispy Imperial Rolls (page 178) or Salt and Pepper Chicken Wings (page 188), and the reality is that if you fry properly, and carefully—as I'll teach you—it's no more messy or smelly or dangerous than any method of cooking.

In Vietnam, fried food is generally not

covered in a thick batter, but simply dusted in cornstarch or flour, which forms a crisp, light coating. It is almost always accompanied with fresh ingredients: crispy duck is paired with watercress, squid is tossed with fresh pineapple, and shrimp fritters are wrapped in lettuce leaves, topped with herbs, and dipped into a bright sauce of fish sauce and lime.

Vegetable oils with a high smoke point and a neutral flavor, such as canola, grapeseed, or peanut, are best for frying. I like to fry in a wok or a large, deep, heavy-bottomed pot, choosing one that is at least twice as deep as the depth of the oil to reduce the risk of a dangerous boil over.

Several years ago, I was reading a recipe for fried chicken in *The Lee Bros. Southern Cookbook*. I have been frying food, including chicken, all my life,

but the Lee brothers' recipe for Sunday fried chicken introduced me to a new frying technique I now consider indispensable: tempering the meat before frying it. By letting the food come to room temperature before adding it to hot oil (just as with any cooking technique for meat), it fries more evenly and more quickly, with the exterior turning a deep golden brown just as the interior reaches doneness.

Deep-frying requires only a few tools, but one of the most essential is a deep-frying thermometer. If you fry a lot, you'll notice the subtle changes in the appearance of the oil as it reaches the proper temperature for frying: the surface will ripple and shimmer just before it begins to smoke, a good indicator of its temperature. But because food fried at a temperature that is too low causes it to absorb oil and become greasy (it spends

more time soaking up oil before it begins to brown), and because some of the more intuitive methods for determining oil temperature are just that, intuitive, you should lay out the twenty dollars and get yourself a reliable thermometer, one that you can clip to the edge of the pot.

Frying in small batches also reduces the likelihood of the food absorbing too much oil. If you add too much food to the pot at one time, the oil temperature will drop dramatically and the food will soak up oil before it begins to brown. Between batches, always let the oil return to the original temperature.

Another handy frying tool is a Chinese 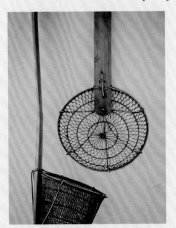 mesh spoon known as a spider, which has a large woven metal bowl and a long bamboo handle. You can use it to turn food and to retrieve it from the oil. Because of its size, it can also support a larger piece of meat (like the whole duck on page 186).

As for the danger of deep-frying: It's really no more dangerous then any cooking technique, but it doesn't hurt to take precautions. If you heat the oil beyond the smoke point, which for canola and peanut oil is around 450°F, it could catch fire. You don't want to walk away from the stove when you're heating oil, and you should always have a lid nearby. If the oil gets too hot, the best thing to do is to cover the pot and remove it from the heat. Never, ever add water to hot oil, which will cause explosive splattering. It's also just good general kitchen practice to keep a small fire extinguisher handy. You'll likely never use it, but it's an inexpensive insurance policy. Get one rated for grease fires. In San Francisco and other progressive urban areas, used frying oil has become a commodity, as more and more people power their cars and cities power their fleets with biodiesel, fuel made from used vegetable oil. All of the vegetable oil we use at the restaurant gets picked up and reused. At home, you can reuse frying oil for several rounds of frying before disposing of it. Let it cool completely after each fry, then strain through a double thickness of cheesecloth into a jar and store in a cool, dark place. You'll know when it's no longer good to use; it will have a rancid flavor and a stale smell.

Fried food in Vietnam is almost always served as part of a meal, not as the main course, and it is almost always accompanied with platters of vegetables and herbs for wrapping, with stir-fried greens, or with a lighter steamed protein. Rarely do the Vietnamese sit down and eat a huge portion of fried food—everything in moderation.

Frying

Imperial Rolls

—

A version of these fried rolls is found on most Vietnamese restaurant menus, and the filling is usually a mixture of pork and shrimp. My version contains both, as well as carrot, jicama, and lightly fried taro root, all of which add texture to the finished rolls. Note that the carrot and jicama need to be salted and left to drain in a colander for at least two hours; you want the filling to be as dry as possible before rolling it up in the rice paper. If it is too wet, the rolls will fall apart when they're fried and the liquid will cause the hot oil to spatter.

Frying them twice makes them extra crispy. The first frying should be done a day ahead: drain the rolls on a double thickness of paper towels between the first and second frying, and refrigerate before you fry them the second time.

- 3 cups finely diced yellow onions
- 1 cup peeled and julienned carrots
- 1 cup julienned jicama (see page 206)
- 2 tablespoons plus 2 teaspoons kosher salt
- Canola oil, for deep-frying
- 3 cups julienned taro root (see page 212)
- 1 (2-ounce) package cellophane noodles (see page 12)
- 12 ounces pork shoulder, finely hand-chopped (see page 52), or ground pork
- 1 cup coarsely chopped shrimp (from about 7 ounces, peeled and deveined)
- 2 teaspoons sugar
- ¼ teaspoon freshly ground black pepper
- 25 (8-inch) rice-paper rounds
- 7 (12-inch) rice-paper rounds, cut into quarters

For Serving
- Red leaf lettuce leaves
- Mint sprigs
- Flavored fish sauce (see page 35), for dipping
- Cooked, cooled vermicelli noodles (see page 12)

Makes 20 to 25 rolls; serves 10 to 12 as an appetizer or snack

1.
In a large bowl, toss together the onions, carrots, jicama, and 2 tablespoons of the salt. Transfer the mixture to a colander and let drain in the sink for 2 hours. Squeeze as much liquid as possible from the vegetables (you can either squeeze them with your hands or roll them tightly in a clean dish towel).

2.
Pour the oil to a depth of 3 inches into a wok or high-sided pot and heat over medium-high heat to 350°F on a deep-frying thermometer. When the oil is hot, add half of the taro and fry for about 7 minutes or until golden brown. Using a spider or a slotted spoon, transfer to paper towels to drain and set aside. Let the oil return to 350° and fry the second batch. Remove the pot of oil from the heat and set aside.

3.
Place the cellophane noodles in a bowl, add very hot water to cover, and let stand for 10 to 15 minutes, until softened. Drain, cut into 2-inch lengths, and set aside.

4.
In a large bowl, combine the onion mixture, fried taro, cellophane noodles, pork, shrimp, sugar, the remaining 2 teaspoons salt, and the pepper and mix well.

5.
Fill a large bowl with very hot water. Working with 1 whole 8-inch rice-paper round at a time, dip it into the hot water until pliable. This will take about 5 seconds. Remove the round from the water and spread it flat on the work surface.

Continued →

Dip one of the quarter rounds of rice paper in the hot water until pliable, then place it on top of the rice-paper round, centering it with the point toward you, to form an area of double thickness.

6.

Place about ¼ cup of the filling on the double thickness of rice paper, spreading it into a rectangle about 3 inches long by 1 inch wide. Lift the bottom edge of the rice-paper round up and over the filling. Roll the rice paper away from you one turn, tightly enclosing the filling completely. Fold in the left and right sides and continue rolling as tightly as possible until you have formed a tight cylinder. Place the roll on a platter or baking sheet and repeat with the remaining rice-paper rounds and filling.

7.

Line a rimmed baking sheet with paper towels and place near the stove. Place a second rimmed baking sheet alongside. Return the pot of oil to medium-high heat and heat the oil to 325°F on the thermometer. When the oil is ready, add 4 or 5 rolls and fry, turning and pressing to submerge them beneath the oil, for 10 to 12 minutes, until lightly browned. Using the spider or slotted spoon, transfer the rolls to the paper towel–lined baking sheet to drain, then transfer to the second baking sheet and let cool completely. Repeat the frying process with the remaining rolls, always allowing the oil to return to temperature between batches. Set the pot of oil aside. Cover the rolls with plastic wrap and refrigerate overnight; bring to room temperature before frying the second time.

8.

When you are ready to serve the rolls, reheat the oil over high heat to 375°F on the thermometer and preheat the oven to 250°F. Line the baking sheet with fresh paper towels. Again working in batches, fry the rolls for 10 minutes, until deep golden brown and crispy. Using the spider or slotted spoon, transfer the rolls to a paper towel–lined baking sheet to drain. Keep warm while you fry the remaining rolls.

9.

Cut each roll in half and place on a platter alongside the lettuce and mint. Pour the fish sauce into small bowls for dipping. To eat, wrap a roll half in a lettuce leaf with some mint leaves and vermicelli, and dip into the fish sauce.

Sweet Potato and Shrimp Fritters

—

These savory fritters originated in Hanoi. Typically, they're made with batons of sweet potato and with shell on shrimp, but because the crunchy shell is something of an acquired taste, I make my fritters with peeled shrimp. The ones pictured opposite are from a restaurant in Vietnam, and were prepared shell on. Like so many fried snacks in Vietnam, the fritters are served with lettuce for wrapping, herb leaves for seasoning, and flavored fish sauce for dipping.

- 1 cup all-purpose flour
- Kosher salt
- ½ teaspoon ground turmeric
- ¼ teaspoon cayenne pepper
- ½ cup thinly sliced scallions, white and light green parts only
- 1 egg, lightly beaten
- 1 cup soda water
- ¼ cup ice water, or as needed
- 18 medium-size shrimp, preferably from the Louisiana Gulf, peeled and deveined
- Pinch of freshly ground black pepper
- 2 pounds sweet potatoes, peeled and cut into 3 by ¼-inch batons (about 5 cups)
- Canola oil, for frying

For Serving
- 18 large red leaf lettuce leaves
- 6 large mint sprigs
- 18 perilla leaves (optional; see page 208)
- ½ cup flavored fish sauce (see page 35)

Makes 18 fritters; serves 6 as a snack

1.
In a bowl, combine the flour, 1½ teaspoons salt, the turmeric, cayenne, scallions, egg, soda water, and ice water and mix just until blended. The batter will be a little lumpy; do not overmix. The texture should be like slightly thin pancake batter. Add more ice water, 1 tablespoon at a time, if it is too thick.

2.
Place the shrimp in a bowl, sprinkle with a pinch of salt and the black pepper, and toss to mix. Pour ½ cup of the batter over the shrimp and toss to coat. Add the sweet potatoes to the bowl holding the remaining batter and stir to mix evenly.

3.
Pour the oil to a depth of ½ inch into a cast-iron frying pan or wok and heat over high heat to 350°F on a deep-frying thermometer. Line a rimmed baking sheet with paper towels, and place a large wire rack on a second baking sheet. Preheat the oven to 250°F.

4.
When the oil is hot, place 5 battered sweet potato batons, side by side, in the oil, taking care to keep them close together. Place 4 or 5 more sweet potato batons on top, perpendicular to the first layer, creating a platform for the shrimp. Make 2 more sweet potato platforms alongside the first platform. Fry the sweet potato platforms for 1 minute, then top each platform with 1 battered shrimp. Spoon a small amount of hot oil over the shrimp to anchor them to the sweet potato batons.

5.
Cook for 2 to 3 minutes more, until the sweet potatoes are golden brown on the first side. Using tongs or a slotted spoon, carefully turn each fritter and cook, shrimp side down, for 1 minute more, until the batter is just set on the second side. Using the tongs or slotted spoon, carefully transfer the fritters to the paper towel–lined baking sheet to drain briefly, then move them to the wire rack and slip them into the oven to keep warm. Repeat with remaining sweet potato batons and shrimp, always allowing the oil to return to temperature between batches.

6.
Arrange the lettuce, mint, and perilla on a platter. Pour the fish sauce into small bowls for dipping. Transfer the fritters to a second platter and season lightly with salt. To eat, wrap a fritter in a lettuce leaf with the herb leaves and dip into the fish sauce.

Squid with Pineapple and Toasted Garlic

—

I went back to Vietnam in the fall of 2011 and ended up at a restaurant—really a shack on the beach—where the beer was ice-cold and the menu was determined by the fisherman's catch. The place had no refrigeration, so the seafood went directly from net to frying pan. I had piles of squid prepared Chinese style: dusted with cornstarch, seasoned with salt and pepper, and fried until crisp.

The sweetness of the pineapple is a perfect counterbalance to the salty fried squid. Use the best fresh, ripe fruit you can find.

- 1½ pounds cleaned squid, bodies and tentacles (see page 157)
- 1 cup cornstarch
- Kosher salt and freshly ground black pepper
- 1 tablespoon canola oil, plus more for deep-frying
- 1½ cups ¼-inch-thick, cored pineapple slices
- 1 tablespoon toasted garlic (see page 25)
- 3 jalapeño chiles, stemmed, seeded, and julienned
- ½ cup coarsely chopped fresh cilantro
- Pinch of sugar

Serves 3 or 4 as an appetizer or part of a multicourse meal

1.
With a sharp knife, slit each squid body length-wise so it lays flat, then slice the body lengthwise into 2 or 3 pieces. In a bowl, combine the pieces with the tentacles and set aside.

2.
In a bowl, stir together the cornstarch, 1 teaspoon salt, and ½ teaspoon pepper and set aside.

3.
In a sauté pan, heat the 1 tablespoon oil over medium heat. When the oil is hot, add the pine-apple slices and cook, turning once, for 3 to 4 minutes on each side, until golden brown. Transfer the pineapple slices to a cutting board, cut into bite-size pieces, then set aside on paper towels to drain.

4.
Pour the oil to a depth of 2 inches into a wok or high-sided pot and heat over high heat to 375°F on a deep-frying thermom-eter. Line a shallow bowl with paper towels. While the oil heats, prepare the squid. Divide the squid into 3 equal portions.

Dredge each portion in the cornstarch mixture, lifting it out with a fine-mesh sieve and shaking off the excess.

5.
When the oil is ready, add one-third of the squid to the hot oil and fry for about 45 seconds, until golden brown and curled. Using a spider or slotted spoon, transfer the squid to the paper towel-lined bowl. Fry the the second and third batches the same way, adding them to the bowl and always allowing the oil to return to temperature between batches. Ten seconds before the last batch of squid is done, add the jalapeño chiles to the hot oil, then remove the chiles from the oil along with the squid.

6.
In a large bowl, combine the fried squid and jalapeños, pineapple, toasted garlic, cilantro, and sugar and toss to combine. Season with salt and pepper and serve immediately.

Frying

Fragrant Crispy Duck with Watercress

—

This recipe is a cousin to the roast duck with crunchy skin and well-done meat you see hanging in shop windows in Chinatown. Making it is a three-step, multiday process: First the duck is brined, then steamed, which helps to render some of the subcutaneous fat. After that, it is plunged into an ice-water bath, which both stops the cooking and tightens the skin. Finally, the duck is double-fried until bronzed and crisp. The best duck to use is the Pekin variety, which has a mild flavor and less fat than the Muscovy.

- 2 cups firmly packed light brown sugar
- 1 cup kosher salt
- 1 (3-inch) piece of Chinese cinnamon (see page 203)
- 8 whole star anise pods (see page 211)
- 2 tablespoons whole cloves
- ½ cup Sichuan peppercorns (see page 211)
- 1 (4-pound) Pekin duck, trimmed of excess fat
- 8 cups ice cubes
- 4 quarts canola oil, for frying
- 1 bunch watercress, tough stems removed

Serves 6 as part of a multicourse meal

1.
In a large, deep stockpot, whisk together 4 quarts cold water, 1 cup of the brown sugar, and the salt until the sugar and salt have dissolved. Set aside.

2.
In a heavy sauté pan, toast the cinnamon, star anise, cloves, and Sichuan peppercorns over medium heat, shaking the pan frequently, for about 2 minutes, until the spices are aromatic. Add the toasted spices to the water–brown sugar mixture. Immerse the duck in the brine, top with a weighted plate to keep the duck submerged, cover, and refrigerate overnight.

3.
Remove the duck from the brine, discard the brine, and wipe away any spices clinging to the duck. Place a roasting pan over two burners on the stove top and pour in water to a depth of 2 inches. Turn on both burners to medium-high heat and set a V-shaped roasting rack in the pan. Put the duck, breast side up, on the rack and cover the roasting pan tightly with aluminum foil. Steam the duck for 30 minutes, checking periodically to ensure water remains in the pan and adding hot water if needed.

4.
When the duck has almost finished steaming, prepare an ice bath. In the stockpot, whisk together 4 quarts water and the remaining 1 cup brown sugar until the sugar has dissolved. Add the ice cubes.

5.
When the duck has steamed for 30 minutes, remove it from the roasting rack and immediately plunge it into the waiting ice bath. Let chill for 5 minutes. Meanwhile, set a wire rack on a rimmed baking sheet. When the 5 minutes have passed, transfer the duck, breast side up, to the wire rack and refrigerate uncovered, for at least 4 hours or up to overnight.

6.
Pour the oil into a large, deep stockpot and heat over high heat to 350°F on a deep-frying thermometer. Line a baking sheet with paper towels and place near the stove. When the oil is ready, carefully lower the duck into the oil, releasing a leg at the last minute so that the oil doesn't splash, and fry for 12 minutes. Using a spider, carefully transfer the duck to the paper towel–lined baking sheet and let stand 15 minutes.

7.
Over high heat, reheat the oil to 375°F. Line a second rimmed baking sheet with paper towels. When the oil is ready, again carefully lower the duck into the oil and fry for 1 to 2 minutes, until the skin is well bronzed and crispy. Using the spider, transfer the duck to the fresh paper towels to drain for a few minutes.

8.
Place the duck, breast side down, on a cutting board. Using poultry shears, cut the backbone from the duck. Then, using a heavy cleaver, chop the duck through the bone into bite-size pieces (see How to Chop a Whole Bird, Asian-Style, page 101, for directions).

9.
Arrange the watercress on a serving platter and top with the duck pieces. Serve immediately.

Salt and Pepper Chicken Wings

—

Fried chicken wings aren't particularly Asian, though they are eaten throughout the continent. But the accompanying lime-salt-chile dipping mixture is a traditional Vietnamese condiment similar to the one served with Shaking Beef (page 140), minus the chile. Salting the wings and leaving them overnight helps season them to the bone. The step is not essential, but it does make a difference. Nothing pairs better with these wings than a cold beer.

- 18 chicken wings, separated at the joints and tips discarded or saved for stock
- Coarse sea salt and coarsely ground black pepper
- 2 Thai chiles, stemmed and minced
- ¼ teaspoon coarsely ground black pepper
- Canola oil, for deep-frying
- ½ cup cornstarch
- 1 tablespoon toasted garlic (see page 25)
- 2 limes, quartered

Serves 6 as an appetizer or part of a multicourse meal

1.
Place the wings in a shallow bowl, sprinkle evenly with 1 tablespoon salt, cover, and refrigerate overnight. The next day, drain the wings in a colander in the sink, then pat dry with paper towels and bring to room temperature.

2.
In a mortar, combine the Thai chiles with 1½ teaspoons salt and grind to a fine paste with a pestle. Transfer to a small bowl and stir in 1½ teaspoons salt and ¼ teaspoon pepper. Set aside.

3.
Pour the oil to a depth of 2 inches into a wok or high-sided pot and heat over high heat to 375°F on a deep-frying thermometer. Line a rimmed baking sheet with paper towels. Preheat the oven to 250°F. While the oil heats, prepare the wings. Put the cornstarch in a bowl and season with a pinch each of salt and pepper. Add the wings and toss to coat with the cornstarch, shaking off any excess.

4.
When the oil is ready, add half the wings to the hot oil and fry for 6 to 8 minutes, until deep golden brown and cooked through. Using a spider or a slotted spoon, transfer the wings to the paper towel–lined baking sheet to drain briefly, then transfer the baking sheet to the oven. Let the oil return to temperature and fry the second batch of wings as directed above. Transfer the second batch to the baking sheet to drain briefly, then transfer all the wings to a bowl, add the toasted garlic, and toss to mix. Season to taste with salt and pepper.

5.
To serve, squeeze the lime juice into the salt-pepper-chile mixture to create a slightly juicy paste. Dip the wings into the paste and eat.

Lacquered Quail with Sichuan Cucumber Pickles

—

This recipe bears some resemblance to recipes for Peking duck and to the recipe on page 186 for Crispy Duck. First the quail are dipped in boiling water that has been seasoned with vinegar and sugar, which tightens the skin and melts some of the subcutaneous fat. Then they are sprinkled with aromatic five-spice salt (five-spice powder, a component of the salt, is a traditional Chinese pairing with poultry) and left to dry for at least a few hours or up to overnight before frying. This treatment results in well-bronzed birds with crispy skin.

I don't like to use boneless quail. They don't cook as evenly as bone-in birds, and for me, part of the fun of eating these quail is gnawing the meat off the bones. This is casual party food but would also make a nice appetizer.

- ½ cup honey
- ½ cup distilled white vinegar
- 2 tablespoons sherry vinegar
- ½ cup firmly packed brown sugar
- 1 teaspoon kosher salt
- 1 (3-inch) piece fresh ginger, crushed
- 6 whole bone-in quail, wing tips removed

Five-Spice Salt
- 2 teaspoons kosher salt
- ¼ teaspoon five-spice powder (see page 205)
- ¼ teaspoon freshly ground black pepper

- Canola oil, for deep-frying

For Serving
- 2 tablespoons coarse sea salt
- 1 teaspoon coarsely cracked black pepper
- 2 limes, quartered
- Sichuan Cucumber Pickles (optional; see page 192)

Serves 6 as a appetizer

1.
In a large saucepan, combine the honey, white vinegar, sherry vinegar, brown sugar, salt, ginger, and 3½ quarts water and bring to a boil over high heat, stirring to dissolve the sugar. Lower the heat so the liquid is at a simmer and simmer for 30 minutes.

2.
Set a wire rack on a rimmed baking sheet. One at a time, submerge each quail in the simmering liquid for 30 seconds, then, using a spider, transfer to the wire rack. Let the quail stand until cool enough to handle. While the quail are cooling, in a small bowl, stir together the kosher salt, five-spice powder, and pepper for the five-spice salt.

3.
Season the cavity of each quail with an equal amount of the five-spice salt. Place the birds on a rimmed baking sheet and refrigerate, uncovered, for at least 6 hours or overnight.

4.
Remove the quail from refrigerator and bring to room temperature. Line a rimmed baking sheet with paper towels. Preheat the oven to 250°F. Pour the oil to a depth of 2 inches into a wok or high-sided pot and heat over medium-high heat to 350°F on a deep-frying thermometer. When the oil is ready, add three of the quail and fry for 5 minutes, until the skin is a deep golden brown. Transfer to the paper towel-lined baking sheet to drain briefly, then transfer the baking sheet to the oven. Let the oil return to temperature and fry the second batch of quail as directed above. Transfer the second batch to the baking sheet to drain briefly.

5.
To serve, using poultry shears, cut the backbone from each quail. Then, with a sharp knife, cut the legs off each quail then cut through the breastbone. Cut each breast through the bone into 3 pieces. Arrange the quail pieces on a platter. In a ramekin, stir together the sea salt and cracked pepper and make a paste for dipping the quail pieces by juicing the limes directly into the salt and pepper mixture. Serve the cucumber pickles on the side.

Sichuan Cucumber Pickles

—

These quick pickles need to sit in vinegar
for only a few hours before you can eat them.
They're great with fried items, since the
vinegar acts as a sort of palate cleanser.
But the ginger, Sichuan peppercorns, and
sambal oelek—a prepared red chile paste that
is readily available at most grocery stores—
make them different than the standard cucumber pickle.

- 1 pound English cucumbers, halved lengthwise
  and cut on the diagonal into ⅛-inch-thick slices
- 2 tablespoons plus 1 teaspoon kosher salt
- 1 (1-inch) piece fresh ginger, peeled and finely
  julienned
- 1 to 2 fresh Thai chiles, stemmed, seeded, and
  julienned
- 4 cups rice vinegar
- 1¼ cups sugar
- 1½ teaspoons sambal chile paste, also known as
  sambal oelek (see page 215)
- ½ cup toasted sesame oil
- 1 tablespoon Sichuan peppercorns (see page 211)
- ¼ cup whole dried red chiles, such as árbol

1.
In a bowl, toss together
the cucumber slices and
1 teaspoon of the salt.
Transfer the cucumbers
to a colander and let
drain in the sink for
2 hours.

2.
Rinse the cucumbers
briefly under cold run-
ning water and drain
well. Transfer to a bowl,
add the ginger and fresh
Thai chiles, and toss
to mix. In a separate
bowl, stir together the
vinegar, sugar, sambal,
and the remaining
2 tablespoons salt until
the sugar and salt have
dissolved. Set aside.

3.
In a small frying pan,
heat the sesame oil over
medium heat. Add the
Sichuan peppercorns
and toast for 10 seconds.
Add the dried chiles
and toast for 10 seconds
longer, until the chiles
darken slightly.

4.
Pour the contents of
the frying pan over the
cucumbers, then add
the vinegar solution and
toss well. Let cool to
room temperature, then
cover and refrigerate.
The pickles are ready to
eat in 2 hours. They will
keep, refrigerated, for
up to 1 week.

Hoi An Wontons with Spicy Tomato Sauce

—

Hoi An is a Vietnamese port town that was an important hub of commerce from the sixteenth through the eigthteenth centuries, particularly for Chinese and Japanese merchants. The local architecture was influenced by the early Chinese settlers, and today the town is filled with old, single-story Chinese shophouses and temples with moss-covered terra-cotta tile roofs—it looks like the set of a kung fu movie. The food here also has a strong Chinese and Japanese influence. You'll find udon noodle soups and Cantonese *char siu* (barbecued pork), as well as these fried pork-and-shrimp wontons.

These are the same wontons that we use in the Wonton Noodle Soup on page 14, but here they are sealed like ravioli for frying.

Tomato Sauce
- 2 tablespoons canola oil
- ¾ cup thinly sliced shallots
- 2 teaspoons minced garlic
- 4 Thai chiles, stemmed and minced
- 2 tablespoons rice wine (see page 215)
- 2 pounds ripe tomatoes (such as Roma or Early Girl), cored and diced
- ¾ cups chicken stock (see page 6)
- 1 tablespoon fish sauce (see page 36)

- 50 square wonton wrappers (1-pound package)
- Pork-and-shrimp wonton filling (see page 14)
- Cornstarch, for dusting
- Canola oil, for deep-frying

Serves 8 to 10 as a snack or appetizer

1.
To make the tomato sauce, in a saucepan, heat the oil over medium heat. Add the shallots and cook, stirring occasionally, for about 3 minutes, until light golden brown. Add garlic and chiles and cook, stirring occasionally, 45 seconds more, until aromatic. Stir in the rice wine, tomatoes, and stock and bring to a boil. Decrease the heat so the mixture is at a gentle simmer and simmer, stirring occasionally, for 45 minutes, to blend the flavors.

2.
Remove the sauce from the heat and stir in the fish sauce. Let cool slightly, then transfer to a blender and process until smooth. Keep warm. (The sauce can be made a day ahead, cooled, covered, and refrigerated; reheat before using.)

3.
To form the wontons, place a wonton wrapper on a work surface. Lightly brush the edges of the wrapper with water and place 1 teaspoon of the filling in the center. Top with a second wonton wrapper, pressing to enclose the filling and form a square, like a ravioli. Force out as much air as possible as you seal the edges to prevent the wontons from puffing up when you fry them. Transfer the finished wontons to a baking sheet or large tray lightly dusted with cornstarch. Repeat until you have used up all of the filling.

4.
Pour the oil to a depth of 2 inches into a wok or high-sided pot and heat over high heat to 375°F on a deep-frying thermometer. Line a rimmed baking sheet with paper towels and place near the stove. Place a second rimmed baking sheet alongside. Preheat the oven to 200°F.

5.
When the oil is ready, add one-third of wontons to the oil and fry for 3 minutes, until deep golden brown and crisp. Using a spider or slotted spoon, transfer to the paper towel–lined baking sheet to drain briefly, then transfer to the second sheet pan and keep warm in the oven. Repeat with remaining wontons in two batches, always allowing the oil to return to temperature between batches.

6.
Arrange the wontons on a platter and serve immediately, accompanied by the tomato sauce. Dip the wontons in the sauce and eat.

Sweet and Sour Fish

—

The first time I went to Thailand, where my wife was born, was for our engagement party. My in-laws hosted a banquet for three hundred people, none of whom I had ever met, prepared by a chef from China. I couldn't tell you what other dishes we had, but the sweet and sour fish will forever stand out in my memory. It's such a simple dish, but the chef exhibited extraordinary artistry: all of the vegetables were perfectly cut, the texture of the fish was silky, and the sauce was rich and slightly reduced so that it coated the fish, rather than gloopy with cornstarch, which is how it is too often made in the States. When made expertly, this is a very special dish. Take the time to cut the vegetables and fry the fish properly. The result is worth the effort.

- 1½ cups chicken stock (see page 6)
- 3 tablespoons freshly squeezed lime juice
- 2 tablespoons distilled white vinegar
- 2 tablespoons fish sauce (see page 36)
- 2 teaspoons sugar
- 1 (1½-pound) whole fish (such branzino or black bass), cleaned, with head and tail intact
- Kosher salt and freshly ground black pepper
- ⅓ cup plus 1 tablespoon cornstarch
- 3 tablespoons canola oil, plus more for deep-frying
- 1 teaspoon finely chopped garlic
- 1 Thai chile, stemmed and minced
- ⅓ cup finely diced yellow onion
- ⅓ cup finely diced celery
- ⅓ cup peeled and finely diced carrot
- ⅓ cup finely diced mango or pineapple
- 2 tablespoons rice wine (see page 215)

Serves 3 or 4 as part of a multicourse meal

1.
In a bowl, stir together the stock, lime juice, vinegar, fish sauce, and sugar until the sugar dissolves. Set aside.

2.
Pour the oil to a depth of 2 inches into a wok or a wide, high-sided sauté pan, and heat over high heat to 350°F on a deep-frying thermometer. While the oil heats, prepare the fish: Rinse the fish, pat dry, and transfer to a cutting board. With a sharp knife, slash the fish on the diagonal 3 or 4 times on each side, cutting all the way to the bone. Season the fish on both sides with ¼ teaspoon salt and ⅛ teaspoon pepper, then dust both sides with ⅓ cup of the cornstarch, brushing off excess. Set aside.

3.
When the oil is ready, holding the fish by its tail, carefully lower it into the hot oil and fry, without turning the fish, for 10 to 12 minutes, until golden brown and just cooked through. Use the tip of a knife to check; the flesh should flake easily. Using a spider, carefully transfer the fish to a warmed platter.

4.
While the fish is frying, make the sauce. In a large sauté pan, heat the remaining 3 tablespoons oil over medium-high heat. When the oil is hot, add the garlic and chile and cook, stirring, for 5 to 10 seconds. Add the onion and cook, stirring, for 1 minute. Add the celery, carrot, and mango and stir to combine. Stir in the rice wine and cook for about 5 minutes, until the vegetables are tender.

5.
Pour the stock mixture into the vegetable mixture. In a small bowl, stir together the remaining 1 tablespoon cornstarch with 1 tablespoon warm water until smooth. Pour this slurry into the sauté pan, stirring to combine. Let cook for 1 minute more, until the sauce thickens.

6.
Pour the vegetables and sauce over the fried fish and serve immediately.

Turmeric-and-Beer-Battered Soft-Shell Crab

—

When I was living in New York after college, I discovered soft-shell crab at Zabar's on the Upper West Side. Since then, I eat them whenever they're in season. I love the contrast of fresh Vietnamese herbs, anchovy-pineapple sauce, and crunchy batter. If you've only ever had soft-shell crabs dusted in flour and fried in butter, try this recipe.

- 6 jumbo live soft-shell crabs
- 1¼ cups all-purpose flour
- 1 cup cornstarch
- 1 tablespoon baking powder
- 2 teaspoons ground turmeric
- 1 teaspoon kosher salt
- ¼ teaspoon cayenne pepper
- 1 egg
- 2 teaspoons balsamic vinegar
- 2 (12-ounce) bottles wheat beer
- Canola oil, for deep-frying

For Serving
- 18 to 24 red leaf lettuce leaves
- 6 large *rau ram* or mint sprigs (see page 210)
- Pineapple-anchovy sauce (see page 56)

Serves 6 as an appetizer

1.
Prepare the crabs: Working with one crab at a time, flip it belly-side up and, with your fingers, pull off the apron (a visible flap opposite the eyes). Flip the crab back over and lift up the shell. On either side, you'll see a feathery bit (the lungs); using your fingers, rip them out. Finally, with a sharp pair of scissors, make a straight cut just behind the eyes.

2.
In a small bowl, stir together the flour, cornstarch, baking powder, turmeric, salt, and cayenne pepper. In a larger bowl, whisk together the egg, vinegar, and 1 bottle of the beer.

3.
Using a rubber spatula, fold the flour mixture into the beer mixture. It should have the consistency of thin pancake batter and may be a little lumpy; do not overmix. Add more beer if needed to achieve the correct consistency. Cover and refrigerate until ready to use.

4.
Pour the oil to a depth of 2 inches into a wok or high-sided pot and heat over high heat to 375°F on a deep-frying thermometer. Line a rimmed baking sheet with paper towels. Preheat the oven to 250°F. When the oil is ready, dip a crab into the batter, allowing the excess to drip off, and then, holding the crab by the shell flaps, carefully lower just the crab legs and body into the hot oil. Wait for 2 seconds, then drop the entire crab into the oil. Repeat with 2 more crabs. Cook for 6 minutes, until golden brown and crispy.

5.
Using a spider, transfer the crab to the paper towel–lined baking sheet to drain, then transfer the baking sheet to the oven to keep warm. Let the oil return to temperature, skimming any bits of batter from the oil with a spider, then fry the remaining three crabs as described above, draining then briefly on a paper towel–lined baking sheet.

6.
Cut each crab in half and arrange the pieces on a large platter, surrounded by the lettuce and *rau ram*. Place the sauce in a bowl alongside. To eat, wrap a piece of crab in a lettuce leaf with some *rau ram* and dip into the sauce.

Frying

Annatto Seeds

These red seeds, harvested from the evergreen annatto tree, are commonly used to color foods, from Cheddar cheese to Mexican soups to chicken tandoori. They have a mild flavor and are usually ground to a powder before using. Although preground annatto is available, the color will be more vibrant if you purchase whole seeds and grind them yourself, either in a mortar with a pestle or in an electric spice grinder. Annatto seeds can be purchased at grocery stores that stock Asian or Mexican ingredients.

Bamboo Shoots

See page 105.

Banana Leaves

Glossy, large, dark green banana leaves are used in Vietnam to wrap dumplings, fish, and meat before steaming or grilling and to line steamer baskets, preventing food from sticking. They are available fresh at some Asian and Latin markets but are more readily available frozen; both are equally good.

Cardamom and Black Cardamon

These pods have a thin papery husk that encloses black seeds and are widely used in Indian and other Southeast Asian cooking. There are two varieties, green and black; green is more common, with a strong, resinous flavor, while the black is found more commonly in Asia and has a slightly smokier flavor. The seed pods are added to dishes whole; when ground cardamom is called for, the seeds must be released from the woody outer husk before being ground. Green cardamom is available in any grocery store's spice section, though you may only find black cardamom in Asian grocery stores or well-stocked spice shops.

Chinese Cinnamon

Though related to "true" Ceylon cinnamon, Chinese cinnamon, which is also called cassia and Saigon cinnamon, comes from an entirely different plant. It's a thick, rough bark which is available both powdered and in stick form; look for sticks that are reddish-orange rather than dark brown, which is a sign of age.

Chinese Sausage

These dried sausages, called *lap cheong* in Cantonese, are sold in links about six inches long. They are deep reddish brown and are typically made from a mixture of pork, pork fat, and sometimes pork liver. You can also find Chinese sausages made of duck liver or even chicken. These sweet, salty links are usually thinly sliced or cubed and added to a pot of rice as it steams, to soups, or to stir-fries.

Ingredients

Curry Leaves

Widely used in the cooking of southern India, these highly fragrant leaves resemble bay leaves, though longer and thinner, and have an unmistakable aroma of curry. They can be found fresh in Asian and Indian groceries and can be frozen in a tightly sealed container for several months. Avoid buying dried curry leaves, which lack the aroma and flavor of fresh.

Daikon Radish

These icicle-shaped white radishes, which can grow up to twenty inches long and are available year-round, have a mild flavor and are often pickled, stir-fried, or grated into soups or salads. Look for firm radishes with no brown spots or cracks that are no longer than a foot with a diameter no greater than 2 inches, as the larger ones tend to be fibrous.

Dried Lily Buds

Lily buds can be found dried, packaged in cellophane, in most Asian grocery stores. They are the buds of tiger lilies—the flowers found in many backyards—and are used primarily to add texture to soups, braises, and stir-fried dishes. They have a powerful smell when dried, which largely dissipates when they are cooked. When buying, look for lily buds that are golden yellow in color; avoid brown buds, which is a sign of age. Before using, soak the dried lily buds in warm water until soft. With a pair of scissors, trim off the fibrous bit at the end of each bud.

Dried Shrimp

Sun-dried shrimp, which are available in various sizes, are used to add savory (*umami*) flavor to dishes throughout Asia, in Central and South America, and in Africa. They are typically soaked in water to soften before use. Some recipes call for pounding the soaked shrimp to a powder and then toasting the powder in a dry skillet. When buying, look for small shrimp with a pinkish color; the best and freshest are found in the refrigerated section of any Asian grocery store. Avoid dried shrimp that are brown or very pale in color, a sign of age.

Five-Spice Powder

This ground spice blend is typically composed of star anise, fennel, Szechuan peppercorns, clove, and cinnamon. When buying, give it a smell—it should have a pronounced aroma, strong enough that you should be able to smell it through the packaging. If it doesn't, don't buy it, as that is a sign of age.

Fermented Black Beans

Sometimes called salted black beans, preserved black beans, or Chinese black beans, these are black beans that have been boiled until soft and then inoculated with mold and preserved in salt. They form the base of black bean sauce, which is frequently paired with seafood and vegetables. Look for plain fermented black beans, the ones without ginger or five-spice powder. Usually sold in plastic sacks or small cardboard drums, they do not need to be rinsed before using.

Fermented Red Bean Curd

These reddish brown tofu cubes, which have been pre-served in a mixture of rice wine, red rice, and salt, are a popular addition to Chinese dishes. The tofu is far too salty and intense to eat on its own, but is often added to marinades and cooked meat dishes and is used in place of shrimp paste (see page 215) in vegetarian dishes. It is sold in glass jars in most Asian grocery stores and must be refrigerated after opening.

Galangal

Also called Siamese ginger, this rhizome is related to ginger but has a spicier, almost bitter flavor. It is frequently used in Thai cooking and less commonly in Vietnamese recipes. Look for chunky knobs that are pale yellow or ivory marked by darker concentric rings. Avoid dried galangal, which lacks flavor. Fresh galangal can be frozen in a resealable plastic bag for up to one month.

Jicama

Although more commonly seen in Latin American cook-ing, jicama, a bulbous root vegetable that is a actually a legume, is also widely used in Southeast Asia kitch-ens and makes a good substitute for fresh water chest-nuts. Peel away the dark brown skin before using.

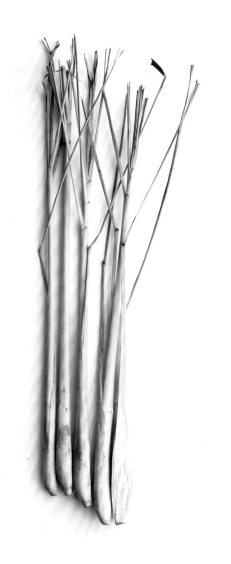

Lemongrass

One of the defining flavors of Vietnamese cooking, lemongrass has an intense lemony smell and taste. The woody, fibrous brown stalks are sold fresh, in bundles, at Asian grocery stores and in many supermarkets. Choose stalks that are about ½ inch in diameter and bend easily; avoid those that seem dry, an indication that they are old. Fresh lemongrass will keep in your refrigerator crisper for several weeks. Whole stalks (and minced lemongrass) can be frozen in an airtight container for several months. Avoid dried lemongrass, which is flavorless. For tips on chopping lemongrass, see page 117.

Mung Beans

Resembling small yellow beads, hulled dried mung beans (which have the outer green hull removed, revealing the yellow interior) are a quick-cooking protein source frequently used in Southeast Asia. You can buy them in bags and in bulk at Asian grocery stores, Indian markets, and some health food stores. Fresh mung bean sprouts (pictured) are readily available in any grocery store. Look for ones that are bright white and crisp and use them within a few days of purchasing.

Palm Sugar

Palm sugar is, as the name indicates, made from the sap of palms, which is boiled down until it crystallizes. It is the sweetener of choice wherever palms are plentiful, including Mexico and Southeast Asia. Usually sold in disks or cones that you can chop or grate, it is golden brown and has a caramelized flavor. Light brown sugar makes a fine substitute; white sugar can also be used.

Perilla

This herb has slightly rounded leaves with a sawtooth edge; there are both green-leafed and purple-leafed varieties. The flavor is minty and lemony. You can find clamshell packages of leaves in well-stocked grocery stores and Asian markets, where they are often labeled with the Japanese name, *shiso*.

Pickled Mustard Greens

See page 119.

Porcini Powder

Made by pulverizing dried porcini mushrooms, this powder is expensive, but a little goes a long way. We use it in combination with dried and fresh mushrooms to give dishes a deep savory flavor. You can find it online or at specialty foods shops. Though most commonly used in Italian dishes, we've co-opted it for the Asian pantry.

Pressed Tofu

To make pressed tofu, fresh tofu is compressed with a weight that pushes out any remaining soy milk and concentrates the curd into a solid block with the consistency of Cheddar cheese. Because of its firm texture, it can be used in stir-fries or grilled. Pressed tofu is sold in blocks and is usually white, though occasionally you'll find dark brown blocks that have been brushed with soy sauce. Both are fine to use. Avoid flavored varieties, however, which are now turning up in supermarkets. If you can't find pressed tofu, you can make your own: wrap extra-firm tofu in cheesecloth, place in a shallow bowl, set a heavy weight on top, and refrigerate for 8 to 12 hours, periodically draining any liquid that accumulates, until liquid stops accumulating and the tofu is firm to the touch.

Preserved Turnip

Made from daikon radish, and also called salted turnip or preserved or salted radish, preserved turnip is sold in translucent bags in most Asian grocery stores. It is pale yellow-gold and is available whole, shredded, or finely minced. For the sake of versatility, I recommend buying it whole and chopping it yourself. It is used to add saltiness and texture to stir-fried dishes, soups, and braises. Once opened, transfer to an airtight container and store in the refrigerator, where it will keep for up to three to four months.

Rau Ram

This green herb, known also as Vietnamese coriander, is widely used in Vietnamese cooking. The leaves are slender and slightly pointed, and the flavor is like a cross between mint and cilantro. It is sold in bunches at Asian markets; look for bunches that are perky and not wilted.

Rice Flour

You can buy rice flour made from plain rice or sweet (glutinous) rice (see page 211). Flour made from plain rice is labeled simply "rice flour" and is made from long-grain white rice. It is used for making noodles, rice paper, and crepes, among other things. Sweet (glutinous) rice flour is generally used for desserts. Both are sold in Asian grocery stores in one-pound bags. Be careful you do not mistakenly pick up sweet rice flour when you want regular rice flour; the packaging is often very similar.

Shiitake Mushrooms

Dried shiitakes are frequently used in braised dishes. They have a more intense flavor than their fresh counterparts and impart a rich, savory flavor to cooked dishes. Fresh and dried shiitakes are graded on a scale of 1 to 3. It's easy to notice the difference when buying fresh—number 1 shiitakes are larger, firm, and unbroken, with intact stems. It's a bit harder to distinguish grades when buying dry mushrooms, but higher quality dried mushrooms will be uniform in size and unbroken, with cross-hatching on the top of each cap. The best come from Japan. Dried mushrooms must be soaked in warm water to rehydrate them before using.

Sichuan Peppercorns

The small reddish brown Sichuan peppercorns are actually berries from the prickly ash tree. They have a incredible aroma and flavor and when, eaten in some quantity, a numbing effect on the mouth.

Star Anise

This reddish-brown star-shaped spice grows on an evergreen tree that is native to China. Star anise has a pronounced anise flavor (though the two are not botanically related) and is widely used throughout Southeast Asia, most typically paired with beef. The eight-pointed stars are added whole to dishes, then removed before serving.

Sweet (Glutinous) Rice

Not to be confused with short-grain rice, sweet rice is a distinct variety that is especially starchy (and available in both long- and short-grain). The raw grains of rice are opaque and when cooked the grains become translucent and very sticky. Sweet rice is typically the rice of choice for desserts and is often combined with savory ingredients, wrapped in banana or lotus leaves and steamed. Both the long- and short-grain varieties of sweet rice can be found at any Asian grocery store; either will work in these recipes.

Tamarind

The sour pulp encased in the pods of the tropical tamarind tree is used in Southeast Asian and Indian cooking, often balanced by sweeter ingredients (or sweetened with sugar). It is sold in cellophane-wrapped reddish black blocks, and though much of the tamarind pulp you find in stores is labeled "seedless," it rarely is. The pulp is typically combined with water or stock and simmered or soaked until softened, then pressed through a fine-mesh sieve as described in the recipes. In Vietnam, tamarind is used in savory dishes and to make sweet-sour candies. It will keep, well wrapped, in the pantry, for up to 6 months.

Tapioca Starch

Also called tapioca flour, this fine powder is made from milling dried cassava root (also known as yuca or manioc). It is used in some dumpling and noodle doughs to give them elasticity, chewiness, and shine, and is added to sauces and soups as a thickener. Look for it in plastic bags in Asian grocery stores.

Taro Root

These hairy tubers are widely used in both Southeast Asian and African cooking, where the starchy root is often a substitute for potatoes. Taro is also a popular crop in Hawaii, where it's boiled and pounded into a paste known as poi. Raw taro can be slightly toxic; if you have sensitive skin, you may want to wear gloves when you peel it. The skin is not edible, so peel taro before using.

Thai Basil

Thai basil resembles Italian basil, but the leaves are often deep green with streaks of purple, and the plants have purple stems. The flavor is more pungent than regular basil, tasting strongly of clove and lemon.

Water Chestnuts

Most people are accustomed to using canned water chestnuts, which have a nice crunchy texture but lack flavor or, worse, have a tinny taste. Fresh water chestnuts are sweet, mild, and crisp. To use, peel off the dark brown outer shell to reveal the sweet white meat. If the interior looks yellow, discard the water chestnut, as it is a sign it is past its prime. If you can't find fresh water chestnuts, jicama (see page 204) makes a good substitute. Look for firm water chestnuts with a dark brown exterior; avoid chestnuts that are soft or have moldy spots.

Yuba (Bean Curd Skins)

Also known as bean curd skins, *yuba* is a by-product of tofu making. When soy milk is warmed, a skin, or sheet, forms on top. These sheets are carefully pulled off the milk and sold fresh or dried, in Asian grocery stores. High in protein, *yuba* is frequently added to Chinese vegetarian dishes. Fresh *yuba* can be used directly from the package; dried *yuba* must be soaked in warm water to soften before using.

Ingredients

Anchovy Fish Sauce
See page 36.

Fish Sauce
See page 36.

Golden Mountain Seasoning Sauce
Also known as mountain soya sauce, this Thai condiment is a soy-based sauce that includes water, salt, and sugar. It is sold in glass bottles, usually with a yellow label and a green cap. Although similar to soy sauce, it has a lighter, sweet flavor. When buying, look for the phrase "naturally fermented" on the label.

Ground Bean Paste
This Chinese condiment, which has a warm brown color and the texture of ketchup, is sold in tins and jars in Asian grocery stores. It is made from naturally fermented soybeans and has a deep savory flavor, similar to brown miso (which can be substituted if you can't find the bean paste). Check the label before buying. The paste is often flavored with garlic or chiles, but a plain version, containing only soybeans, water, salt and sugar, is preferred. Refrigerate the paste after opening; it will keep for many months.

Maggi Seasoning Sauce
This popular vegetable protein-based condiment, used throughout the world and especially popular in Southeast Asia, was invented by a Swiss company in the 1800s as a substitute for meat extract. Although it does not contain soy, it is similar in taste and consistency to soy sauce. In Vietnam, the condiment is used to finish noodle dishes and is liberally sprinkled on the filling for *bánh mì*.

Oyster Sauce
This deep brown Chinese seasoning is made from oyster extract, sugar, salt, and cornstarch; occasionally soy sauce is added. It has a rich, sweet-savory flavor and is typically added to stir-fried dishes, and is often combined with rice wine, sugar, cornstarch, and other ingredients to make a slightly thickened sauce for vegetables and fish. A vegetarian version (with mushrooms standing in for the oysters) is also available; see vegetarian stir-fry sauce.

Rice Wine

The best rice wine is made in the Chinese town of Shaoxing, in Zhejiang Province. It has a golden color and a nutty, sweet flavor. It is frequently added to stir-fries, sauces, and braises. It is available in some liquor stores and in Asian grocery stores. If you can't find it, dry sherry is an acceptable substitute.

Roasted Chile Paste

See page 117.

Sambal Chile Paste/Sambal Oelek

This is a Southeast Asian condiment that is, at its most basic, a blend of red chiles, water, and salt. Other versions contain lime juice, garlic, and lemongrass; some contain dried anchovies and shrimp paste. It is sold in plastic jars in Asian grocery stores. We recommend the most basic version; you can always enhance it at home with fresh ingredients.

Shrimp Paste

Sold in jars, this pinkish gray condiment is made from fermented salted shrimp. It has a pungent, salty flavor and is frequently mixed with lime juice and sugar, which tempers its strong taste.

Soy Sauce

This naturally brewed condiment is made from fermented soybeans that have been mixed with wheat, water, and salt. Dark soy sauce is thicker, darker, and less salty than light soy sauce and has been fermented for a shorter period of time. Light soy sauce, also known as thin soy, is lighter in both flavor and texture. In general, Chinese-made soy sauces tend to be saltier than Japanese brands (called *shoyu*).

Vegetarian Stir-Fry Sauce

Often labeled "vegetarian oyster sauce," this is a vegetarian alternative to traditional oyster sauce, with shiitake mushrooms standing in for the oysters. It is deep brown and has a rich, savory-sweet flavor. Check the label before buying; lesser companies often boost the flavor of their sauce with MSG. Once opened, it will keep, refrigerated, for many months. See also oyster sauce.

Acknowledgments

—

Without the help and patience of the following people, you would not be reading this book.

Many thanks to my agent and dear friend, Katherine Cowles, who helped escort me into and guide me through the book writing world.

A thousand thanks to my writer, Jessica Battilana, who had to listen to thousands of stories and somehow managed to turn those stories into this book.

Friend and photographer Eric Wolfinger not only has a fantastic eye and patience, he also has an iron stomach, which was put to the test when we traveled together in Vietnam.

I was fortunate enough to meet Tom and Patricia Crabtree of Manual Creative, who brought a wonderful aesthetic to the book design.

At Ten Speed, gratitude and appreciation to my editors Jenny Wapner and Aaron Wehner who believed in this project and supported me in my quest to make a truly unique book.

Thank you to my in-house book team: Justine Kelly, Slanted Door chef de cuisine, and Lien Lin, Slanted Door sous chef, who logged many long hours developing, testing and retesting (and retesting again) recipes, despite their many other daily duties at the restaurant. And thank you to my aunt, Phai Pham, who has an encyclopedic knowledge of classic Vietnamese recipes.

I also want to thank my dear friend Olle Lundberg and his wife Mary Breuer. Olle, you have always inspired me to do better and believe in myself.

Of course, many thanks to my family, starting with my wife Angkana and my children, brothers and sisters, in-laws, and mother and father.

Lastly, thank you to all our staff at the Slanted Door Group restaurants, who all contributed, whether directly or indirectly, to this book.

Measurement Conversion Charts

—

Volume

U.S.	Imperial	Metric
1 tablespoon	½ fl oz	15 ml
2 tablespoons	1 fl oz	30 ml
¼ cup	2 fl oz	60 ml
⅓ cup	3 fl oz	90 ml
½ cup	4 fl oz	120 ml
⅔ cup	5 fl oz (¼ pint)	150 ml
¾ cup	6 fl oz	180 ml
1 cup	8 fl oz (⅓ pint)	240 ml
1¼ cups	10 fl oz (½ pint)	300 ml
2 cups (1 pint)	16 fl oz (⅔ pint)	480 ml
2½ cups	20 fl oz (1 pint)	600 ml
1 quart	32 fl oz (1⅔ pint)	1 liter

Temperature

Farenheit	Celsius/Gas Mark
250°F	250°C/gas mark ½
275°F	135°C/gas mark 1
300°F	150°C/gas mark 2
325°F	160°C/gas mark 3
350°F	180 or 175°C/gas mark 4
375°F	190°C/gas mark 5
400°F	200°C/gas mark 6
425°F	220°C/gas mark 7
450°F	230°C/gas mark 8
475°F	245°C/gas mark 9
500°F	260°C

Length

Inch	Metric
¼ inch	6mm
½ inch	1.25 cm
¾ inch	2 cm
1 inch	2.5 cm
6 inches (½ foot)	15 cm
12 inches (1 foot)	30 cm

Weight

U.S./Imperial	Metric
½ oz	15 g
1 oz	30 g
2 oz	60 g
¼ lb	115 g
⅓ lb	150 g
½ lb	225 g
¾ lb	350 g
1 lb	450 g

Index
—